Scrapbook for Chinese Collectors

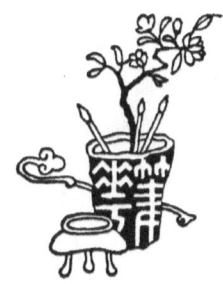

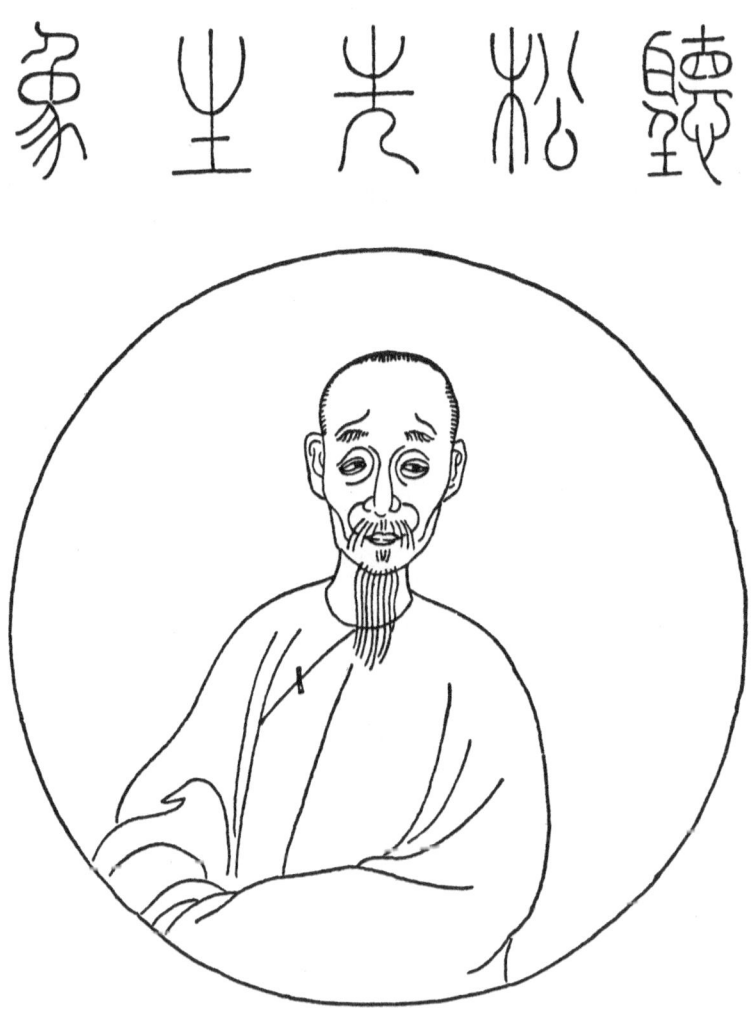

The Chinese connoisseur and bibliophile Lu Shih-hua (1714-1779)

Scrapbook for Chinese Collectors

A Chinese Treatise on Scrolls and Forgers

Shu Hua Shuo Ling

Translated with commentary by
R. H. van Gulik, LITT. D.

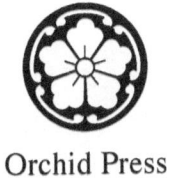

Orchid Press

SCRAPBOOK FOR CHINESE COLLECTORS: A Chinese Treatise on Scrolls and Forgers
Shu Hua Shuo Ling
Translated with commentary by R. H. van Gulik

First published privately in Beirut, 1958

Reprint edition, 2006

ORCHID PRESS
P.O. Box 19,
Yuttitham Post Office,
Bangkok 10907 Thailand
www.orchidbooks.com

Copyright © Estate of R. H. van Gulik. Protected by copyright under the terms of the International Copyright Union: all rights reserved. No part of this publication may be reproduced in any form or by any means, electronic or mechanical, including photocopying, recording, or by any information storage or retrieval system without prior permission in writing from the publisher.

Cover illustration from *Shizhuzhai Jianpu* (Decorative Letter Papers from the Ten Bamboo Studio); Rongbaozhai, Beijing 1952.

ISBN 978-974-524-081-0

While writing my book "Chinese Pictorial Art", now printing in the Italian Institute for Middle and Far Eastern Studies in Rome, I often quoted the Scrapbook left by the 18th century collector Lu Shih-hua. There I translated in total about one-fifth of his treatise.

However, only a complete translation can do full justice to this Scrapbook, which is an original contribution to the study of Chinese pictorial art, written by a discerning Chinese connoisseur who devoted a lifetime to the collecting of antique books and pictures. Hence his Scrapbook is presented here in a complete translation, together with an introduction, notes, and a reprint of the Chinese text.

My thanks are due to Mr. K.T.Wu of the Library of Congress in Washington D.C., who kindly sent me a photostat of Lu Shih-hua's biography, and to Mr. J. L. Cranmer-Byng of the University of Hongkong who had the Chinese text printed for me.

Beirut, Spring 1958   *R.H.v.G.*

The design on the half-title page (p. 1), a brush holder with three brushes and a flowering branch, accompanied by an incense burner and a sceptre—symbol of quiet enjoyment of life—represents the Chinese expression pi-t'ou-sheng-hua *"flowers blossoming from the brush", originally referring to the famous T'ang poet Li Po, but later used for literary and artistic activities in general.*

INTRODUCTION

Chinese books, treatises and essays on pictorial art and its appreciation published in the 18th and 19th century are counted by the hundred, and many bear the names of famous scholars. The question arises why the Scrapbook of Lu Shih-hua, a minor collector and bibliophile, was selected here for translation.

In order to explain this choice, we must briefly review conditions obtaining in the field of artistic studies in Lu Shih-hua's time.

In the Ch'ing dynasty art-criticism had settled down into a rut. An artistic tradition of nearly fifteen centuries had developed a technical terminology for the connoisseurship of pictorial art that dominated all literature on the sister-arts of calligraphy and painting. This terminology was derived from a set of generally accepted old standard texts. Ch'ing literati when using this terminology had perforce to adopt together with it the ideas expressed in those older works. For in the

Ch'ing dynasty the Chinese literary language had become so bound by terminology and stylistic precedent that writers were finding it increasingly difficult to phrase entirely new thoughts on old, traditional subjects — and still write good Chinese.

As a matter of course this difficulty was inherent only in the literary language. But in Lu Shih-hua's time all serious literature had to be written in that idiom—nearly two hundred years were to elapse before the Literary Renaissance would assign to the colloquial its rightful place in literature.

A rigid tradition circumscribed not only the form, but also the substance of art-critical studies. It was generally accepted that the antique autographs and paintings set a standard for all times, and the so-called *ming-chi* were considered the cream of those. A *ming-chi*, literally "famous scroll," is a superior specimen of the work of a great ancient master, preserved in fair condition, and the antecedents of which are reliably known.

In Lu Shih-hua's time practically all existing *ming-chi* had been placed on record, they bore the names of most of the great painters and calligraphers from ca. the 4th till the 14th century. The majority were preserved in the Palace Collection, the rest was in the hands of some leading families and great col-

INTRODUCTION 9

lectors. Tradition decreed that these antique paintings and autographs* were the highest expression of Chinese pictorial art, and to cast doubt on their quality and authenticity was considered to be nearly sacrilegious.

As a matter of fact, however, these *ming-chi* were of very mixed quality. In the course of the centuries famous works of art had undergone so many vicissitudes, and copyists and forgers had so diligently plied their trade, that in the Ch'ing dynasty only a small number of those scrolls could be considered as above all doubt. Many serious connoisseurs realized this situation, but few dared to discuss it openly. Times had greatly changed after the 12th century, when critically-minded connoisseurs like the great scholar-artist Mi Fu (1051-1107 A.D.) could freely voice their iconoclastic views on the authenticity of well-known autographs and paintings. China was now ruled by the alien Manchu dynasty, and one had to think twice before writing down anything that could in any way be construed as reflecting on the knowledge and taste of the rulers. Not a few

---

* The term "autograph" is used throughout this book as a translation of the Chinese term *shu*, in its meaning of a shorter or longer specimen of handwriting, the value of which lies in the quality of the calligraphy rather than in the content of the text written out.

literati who did so were summarily executed together with their entire family.

And as to other antique paintings and autographs circulating in Lu Shih-hua's time, the situation was even worse. Although good old scrolls were few and mostly in fixed hands, the owning of a few works by old masters had become such an integral part of cultured life that every person with social pretensions had to have some of them. They belonged, so to speak, to the furniture of every upper middle-class house, just like a piano with us. Every high official, every wealthy merchant wanted to display some antique scrolls in his hall. And those had to bear the signatures of only the greatest of the old masters, for it were only those that most of the proud owners were familiar with. Since thus the demand for antique scrolls was enormous and the supply short, prices of autographs and pictures rose to a fantastic height, while their quality declined. The trade of the forger flourished as never before, and shady dealers did a thriving business in old and new copies and fakes.

These facts also were well known to serious collectors and art-critics, but here again tradition imposed silence. For the writing about the tricks of forgers and crooked dealers was considered intolerably vulgar, and

INTRODUCTION 11

wholly incompatible with the elementary dictates of literary elegance.

Thus most writers on pictorial art of that time preferred to pass over in discreet silence those dangerous or inelegant aspects of their subject.

Lu Shih-hua, the connoisseur who in 1776 A.D. wrote the present Scrapbook, is one of the rare exceptions. He was an ardent lover of pictorial art who devoted a life time to the building up of a collection of antique and later autographs and paintings. At the same time he was a man of a critical and inquiring turn of mind. In his Scrapbook he attempted to express his individual views on the appraising, collecting and displaying of antique pictures, basing himself upon extensive data gathered in Soochow and nearby cities —a region which for centuries past had been a centre of the antique trade. He expressed his ideas in a vigorous prose, denouncing the hackneyed piece-work produced by many Ming and Ch'ing writers on those subjects as plain plagiarism. In doing so he eluded the limitations imposed by literary tradition by coining his own terminology, often making use of colloquial expressions. Being an excellent stylist, he could mix the literary and colloquial idioms and still write good prose, and use new terms and still avoid ambiguity. He set down his doubts regarding the *ming-chi* and his disapproval of the exaggerated veneration for the old masters whose miraculous talents had developed into a kind of myth. At the same time he expressed in unequivocal terms his contempt of ignorant collectors who could not "distinguish a deer from a horse" and moreover evinced atrocious taste in displaying their pictures. Finally he sharply denounced the tricks of forgers and crooked dealers.

Therefore Lu Shih-hua's Scrapbook, brief though it is, rises head and shoulders above most larger works of a similar nature written at that time. Its merits were recognised by the eminent bibliophile Hsü Tseng (1824-1903 A.D.), who reprinted it in his collection *Yü-yüan-ts'ung-k'o*.*

If one adds thereto that Lu Shih-hua was a man of a warm-hearted disposition gifted with a kind of wry humour, I hope that the reasons which prompted a separate translation of his Scrapbook will be sufficiently clear.

* * *

---

* The Chinese text printed after the translation is based on that of Hsü Tseng, but the punctuation is added by me.

INTRODUCTION 13

Lu Shih-hua was born in 1724 A.D. in T'ai-ts'ang, a small city in the lake district of Kiangsu Province, to the NW of Shanghai, but he seems to have passed the greater part of his life in nearby Soochow, a city famous for its scenic beauty, and since centuries past the home of scholars, artists and art-dealers.

He belonged to a prominent local family, and was apparently a man of independent means who never occupied an official position. The authorities, however, often charged him with the supervision of public works the execution of which implied the handling of large government funds; his biography mentions the construction of dykes, sluices and bridges. This proves that he was a man of unquestioned integrity, for it was the execution of such works that gave corrupt officials ample opportunity for lining their pockets to the detriment of public interest. When in 1757 the Emperor Ch'ien-lung made his tour of Kiangsu and Chekiang Province, Lu Shih-hua was charged with preparing the Emperor's temporary residence. He further engaged in various charitable works, and also restored a famous old Buddhist temple. He died in 1779 A.D. from some disease of the respiratory organs (*ch'uan*), perhaps asthma.

These meagre details of what apparently was a

fairly uneventful life are gathered from Lu Shih-hua's tomb inscription, written by the famous poet, scholar and statesman Wang Ch'ang (1725-1806 A.D.), and printed in ch. 438 of the large biographical work *Kuo-ch'ao-ch'i-hsien-lei-cheng*.

This tomb-inscription could not well mention one important fact which throws an interesting sidelight on Lu Shih-hua's personality. That is that during the literary inquisition conducted in 1772-1788 on the orders of the Emperor Ch'ien-lung, Lu Shih-hua's catalogue of scrolls was placed on the Index.* As I explained in my note 5 on page 70 below, this was doubtless due to a passage in Chapter I of his Scrapbook where he expresses his disapproval of the alien Manchu rule. This proves that Lu Shih-hua, apart from being an excellent art-critic, also was a fervent Chinese patriot.

The Frontispiece of the present publication is a portrait of Lu Shih-hua, traced after a woodcut appearing in the *Wu-yüeh-ming-jen-hua-hsiang*, a small 19th century illustrated work on well-known persons from

---

* Cf. L. Carrington Goodrich, *The Literary Inquisition of Ch'ien-lung*, American Council of Learned Societies, Studies in Chinese and related civilizations, No. 1, Baltimore 1935, page 251.

S. Kiangsu and N. Chekiang. As a rule traditional Chinese portrait painters pay more attention to the type they wish to reproduce than to giving a good likeness, while also the laws of physiognomy play a large role. Since in this case, however, the book was published fairly soon after Lu Shih-hua's time, there is a chance that the portrait shows his real features.

Apparently the only published work Lu Shih-hua left is a descriptive catalogue of his own collection of autographs and paintings, including also works he had seen elsewhere. He had this book printed in 1777, under the title *Wu-yüeh-so-chien-shu-hua-lu*, "Catalogue of Autographs and Paintings seen in Wu-yüeh," in six chapters. The term Wu-yüeh designates the southern part of Kiangsu and the northern part of Chekiang, a region since olden times famous as a centre of artistic life, where many of the great Chinese painters and writers lived and worked. Although in Chapter XII of his Scrapbook Lu Shih-hua speaks disparagingly about the number and quality of the scrolls he listed, the book contains in fact careful descriptions of more than 600 interesting items. Ch. 1-5 are devoted to scrolls of the T'ang, Sung, Yüan and Ming dynasties, about 500 items; ch. 6 deals with works of the Ch'ing period, about 180 items. In 1910 this catalogue was reprinted under the auspices of the modern art-historian Teng Shih, with a preface by the literatus Chiang Piao (1860-1899), dated 1879; this second edition I have not seen.

The Scrapbook translated here is a brief collection of 29 notes on pictorial art, greatly varying in length and content, and printed by Lu Shih-hua at the beginning of his catalogue, as a kind of introduction. He had written it one year previously, in 1776 A.D., and given it the title of *Shu-hua-shuo-ling*. "Shu-hua" means autographs and paintings, while "shuo-ling" is a self-deprecatory expression meaning literally "sayings tinkling softly like small bells." Thus the title of the Scrapbook might be translated as "Insignificant Observations on Autographs and Paintings."

At the end of the catalogue Lu Shih-hua added a brief postscript, entitled *Shu-hua-tso-wei-jih-ch'i-lun* "On the daily increasing eccentricities of scroll-forgers." Since this postscript supplements his remarks on fakes and forgeries contained in the Scrapbook, I have added a translation at the end of this Introduction. The Chinese text is reproduced after that of the Scrapbook.

As was pointed out above, to publish such a treatise on pictorial art that went right against the stream, asked for considerable courage. It is true that Lu Shih-hua did not occupy an official position, and thus was less vulnerable than many a high official on a responsible post. Yet he had to be careful. He did not mince words in exposing the knavery of shady art-dealers, untrustworthy mounters and crooked brokers in his district; he reveals that often they colluded with wineshop owners and brothel keepers, joining hands in cleaning out wealthy customers and unwary travelers bent on either the spiritual or the physical enjoyment of beauty —or both. But those enterprising gentlemen formed a powerful business-organization, and they could be dangerous enemies. Also his caustic criticism of ignorant and snobbish collectors might easily be taken by one or another influential person as directed against himself. Generally speaking the Chinese social pattern was such a complex one that when publishing strong views that deviated from the approved pattern, one never knew what person one might offend and how that person might take his revenge. Therefore Lu Shih-hua could not serve up his treatise without a certain amount of "dressing."

The reader must see the Preface and Chapter I of the Scrapbook in this light. The Preface—rather forbidding as most Chinese prefaces—is intended to prepare the conventional reader for the unconventional content. In Chapter I he borrows a passage from a lesser known ancient writer as a frame work for formulating his doubts regarding the *ming-chi*, his disapproval of the sterile art-critical discussions of most contemporary writers, and his contempt of unscrupulous and fraudulent dealers.

After these preliminaries, however, he takes us straight to the subject-matter. In Chapters II and III he says a few words about the arrangement of his catalogue, and points out that whereas former collectors limited their interest to famous antique scrolls, he was quite content with lesser items, and works of later date. Here it should be added that this idea in itself was not a new one. Similar thoughts were voiced already in the 12th century by the Sung connoisseur Chao Hsi-ku, who observes in his *Tung-t'ien-ch'ing-lu-chi*: "Remote indeed are the men of olden times. Although Ts'ao Chung-ta (flourished ca.600 A.D.) and Wu Tao-tzu (fl.ca.750 A.D.) are men of fairly recent times, not one single painting by them has been preserved. How then could one ever hope to see scrolls by Ku K'ai-chih (4th century), Lu T'an-wei (5th century) or other artists of their period? Therefore, when discussing paintings one had better take as standard those pictures one can actually see. For if one persists in referring to old artists, saying 'This is a Ku K'ai-chih,' or 'This is a Lu T'an-wei,' one not only deceives others, but in fact also himself!"

But Lu Shih-hua goes further than that. In Chapter V he even maintains that leading Ch'ing painters did better work than the celebrated ancients. This was a revolutionary statement, liable to elicit severe criticism.

Chapter VI is a brilliant analysis of the principles for judging paintings, evidently the result of much mature thought on this delicate subject.

Here the reader will notice that Lu Shih-hua treats originals and copies on the same footing. As a matter of fact the traditional Chinese view of authenticity is fundamentally different from ours. While we insist that a picture actually is painted by the man whose signature it bears or whom it is ascribed to, the Chinese have throughout the centuries considered this as a point of secondary importance; for them works of art serve in the first place to preserve and faithfully transmit the spirit of the artists, they did not particularly care whether this aim was achieved by originals or by good, bona-fide copies. Already during the T'ang and Sung dynasties the works of great masters of the preceding periods were carefully copied in the Imperial Palace, and listed and preserved as carefully as original paintings. Chinese connoisseurs do object, however, to bad copies, and especially to copies made expressly for being sold as originals. It is only such copies that are called *wei-tso*, "forgeries," and it is on such that Lu Shih-hua in other chapters of his Scrapbook pours out his vials of wrath.

Lu Shih-hua adopts a lighter vein in Chapters VII-XI, where he wittily describes the joys and vexations that fall to the lot of a collector. In each of these chapters he first describes a pleasant occurrence, then narrating a less fortunate incident which he designates as "a tremendous nuisance." These notes are based on personal experience, and many of the exasperating characters introduced are evidently drawn from life.

In Chapter XII Lu Shih-hua once more warns against concentrating on antique specimens, and in Chapter XIII turns against those collectors who care only for very rare and perfect items. Chapter XIV discusses the bad habits of some collectors who indiscriminately add seals and inscriptions to antique scrolls.

Chapters XV-XX describe in a vivid style some tricks of crooked dealers and forgers of antique paintings; Chapter XX sums up his own experiences in the Wu-yüeh region.

Chapters XXI and XXII discuss the relative importance of seals and signatures, and Chapter XXIII

INTRODUCTION

points out the necessity of storing antique specimens away safely, and of having them repaired only by the best experts.

In Chapters XXIV-XXVII Lu Shih-hua again takes to task crooked dealers; he describes the correct methods for showing scrolls and for storing them; and he also gives advice on how they should be displayed.

The treatise closes with some sharp remarks on ignorant collectors and soi-disant connoisseurs.

* * *

Since the present publication is primarily intended for the general reader, I did not want to burden my translation with footnotes. Names, booktitles and a few literary allusions and technical terms will be found explained in the notes, added after the translation. It may not be superfluous, however, to explain here in a few words how Chinese autographs and paintings are mounted, since a general knowledge thereof is indispensable for following Lu Shih-hua's argument.*

---

* The reader will find more details about the art of mounting, and on the problems of Chinese connoisseurship in general, in my book *Chinese Pictorial Art as viewed by the Connoisseur*, Notes on the means and methods of traditional Chinese connoisseurship based upon a study of the art of mounting scrolls in China and Japan, Rome 1958.

The majority of autographs and paintings are mounted either as hand scrolls (Chinese *shou-chüan*, Japanese *makimono*), or hanging scrolls (Chinese *kua-fu*, Japanese *kakemono*). There exist also other types of mounting such as albums, tablets, etc. but those form the minority, and Lu Shih-hua does not mention them in his Scrapbook.

A hand scroll is an autograph or painting mounted on a long horizontal strip of silk or paper. At the end of the scroll, that is on the extreme left, there is attached a wooden roller for winding the scroll round when it is stored away. Hand scrolls are not used in interior decoration, they are viewed while being unrolled on the desk. A hanging scroll can be described as a hand scroll turned round 180 degrees; the roller at the bottom serves not only to wind the scroll round when stored away, but also as a stretcher when it is hanging on the wall. Unlike the hand scroll, the hanging scroll can be left on display for a length of time, and hence plays an important role in Chinese interior decoration.

When an autograph or painting is mounted it is first provided with a backing, then surrounded on all four sides with a kind of frame consisting of strips of paper, silk or brocade. The mounting serves to protect and embellish the picture, and thus can to a certain extent be compared with our Western picture-frame. But a Chinese mounting is not an easily detachable, temporary addition. It forms one with the picture, and can be detached only by a complicated and laborious process; especially in the case of antique paintings this process involves great risks and clumsy mounters may ruin a picture for ever. Hence Lu Shih-hua advises to leave damaged scrolls as they are if one can not find a really good mounter (see Chapter XXIII), a statement that echos similar warnings by T'ang and Sung connoisseurs. One need not wonder, therefore, that mounters played a predominant role in Chinese artistic life.

Most pre-T'ang autographs and paintings are mounted as hand scrolls, for the hanging scroll mounting became popular only during that period. Hand scrolls are mounted with one or more extra-sheets of blank paper at the beginning and end, separated from the picture itself by narrow vertical strips of mounting material. Connoisseurs and collectors write there their notes and comments. Those at the beginning of the scroll—or on the picture itself—are called *t'i* "superscriptions," those at the end *po* (colloquial *pa*), i.e. "colophons." Most antique scrolls have scores of *t'i-po* attached to them; these are of great importance for the study of the antecedents and authenticity of the painting they are attached to, they are mentioned already by connoisseurs of the T'ang dynasty. To prevent the *t'i-po* from going astray when the scroll is remounted, collectors usually stamp their seals over the seams; these seals are hence called *ch'i-feng-yin* "seals astride the seams." Despite these and other safeguards, however, crooked dealers will play all kinds of tricks with detached or stray *t'i-po*—as described by Lu Shih-hua in Chapter XI of his Scrapbook.

Hanging scrolls are as a rule not mounted with an extra blank space for writing comments. Collectors often write their notes on the picture itself, or on the silk or paper of the front mounting—as is done also occasionally in the case of pictures mounted as hand scrolls. In Chapter XIV Lu Shih-hua points out that location, style and spacing of such inscriptions directly written on the picture should be chosen with special care. The same applies to the adding of seals to autographs and paintings.

* * *

Finally, there may be added a few words on Lu Shih-hua's scathing denunciation of unscrupulous art dealers.

For a correct appreciation of his remarks one must remember that Lu Shih-hua lived in one of the great artistic centres of China, where the antique trade had been flourishing since centuries, and where also its seamy side was naturally specially thriving. Since other writers were wont to pass over these less creditable aspects in silence, Lu Shih-hua felt duty-bound to lay considerable stress on them. It is indeed useful to bear in mind that the forging of scrolls was practised on a large scale, and that many curio dealers took an active part in this deceit. One must not forget either, however, that although the history of copying, faking and forging of autographs and paintings goes back as far as the fifth century A.D. there are, then as now, uncounted antique dealers who will have no truck with forgers and who are as honest as can be expected of people engaged in a business of greatly varying returns and fluctuating profits.

This reserve made, it is worth while to translate here the Postscript that Lu Shih-hua added to his catalogue.

On the daily increasing eccentricities of scroll-forgers.

"The forging of pictures and autographs has been practised since olden times. Often the forger would make uncounted close and free copies of an original, hoping by doing so to grasp the spirit of the artist's brush-work. But as a result the forger, having started by being unfamiliar with the artist's work, ends up by being too familiar with it; whereas his first copies were close to the original, his later ones are remote from it, so that they can be easily detected.

"If one finds a famous scroll with many colophons and superscriptions (signed by different persons) attached to it, one will notice that all of those were copied by the same hand; although the forger did his utmost to vary his brush-technique (for each item), his work will still betray his own individuality.

"The people of old used things sparingly, keeping to the minimum needed, and also forgers did not like to use good ink, valuable paper and selected brushes. They would forge old pictures on new silk and paper, an inconsistency which strikes the observer at once and makes further tests superfluous.

"At present forgers do not copy old works, they do not write the names of famous masters on their fakes, but choose only lesser-known artists, and they even succeed in bestowing on such fakes an appearance of spontaneity. Such fakes cannot be tested by comparing them with original works (by the alleged artist) or with rubbings (of that artist's works engraved in stone).

They also take good care to vary (the calligraphy) of the superscriptions and colophons (which they attach to such a fake), writing them alternately in regular, draft, chancery or seal script, so as not to betray (their being written by the same person). Or also they will have these inscriptions written by a number of people, to show convincing differences (in the calligraphy).

"Sūtra-paper* and paper of the Hsüan-te period (1426-1435) is now rare, forgers will write recklessly large characters right across the tears in sheets of such old paper, so that the characters show lacunae (which adds to the antique flavour of such fakes).

"Collector's seals of connoisseurs of former times, and seals bearing the names and appellations of famous people, can often still be found. Forgers will borrow those seals and impress them on the seams of their fakes, which they have moreover mounted in a most

---

* *Tsang-ching-chih*, a glazed, light-brown paper. Also called *Chin-su-chih* "Paper from the Chin-su Temple," because in that temple, located near Hai-yen, there was preserved a copy of the Buddhist Canon dating from the T'ang dynasty and written on this superior paper. Since early times its stray leaves were used by mounters for making the title-labels and superscriptions of valuable scrolls. The original paper is rare, but its name is applied to an imitation, a yellow paper with brown spots, popularly called *hu-p'i-chih* "tiger-skin paper," and today still widely used for the title labels of books and scrolls.

luxurious manner, "with title-labels written in gold and jade roller knobs." They will go to the greatest trouble in thinking out such tricks, but thereby only betray their mean character.

"But stranger still is the fact that experienced and honest connoisseurs often unwittingly promote the production of forgeries. When Kao Shih-ch'i compiled his *Hsiao-hsia-lu* (the catalogue of antique scrolls mentioned on page 74 below) he recorded in detail the size of each item, and the seal impressions occurring on it, so as to put an end to the wiles of crafty dealers. But as a result present-day forgers give their fakes exactly the same measurements as recorded in the catalogue, and they can imitate the legends of the seals reproduced there. They do not refer to the original autographs and paintings described by Kao Shih-ch'i, but arbitrarily write or paint something according to their fancy. The forgers have no opportunity for seeing the original scrolls recorded in Kao's catalogue, but neither have the prospective buyers! Thus they can do as they like, in the hope that the buyers are satisfied when upon consulting Kao's catalogue they find that the measurements of the fakes tally exactly.

"Some dealers go even as far as to pose as descendants of Kao Shih-ch'i or of (the great Ming collector)

Hsiang Yüan-pien (1525-1590), they learn to speak with a Kiangsu or Chekiang accent (Kao was a native of Hangchow, Hsiang of Kashing. Transl.), and thus try to pass off their fakes as items emanating from those famous old collections. Others again draw well-known collectors in their plot and obtain permission to deposit their own fakes in their houses. Then they take prospective customers there to view the pictures, thus convincing them that it must be rare treasures.

"Alas, the people of old, besides firmly establishing for all time their virtuous and meritorious deeds and their wise teachings*, also engaged in the arts of calligraphy and painting, thereby leaving monuments of enduring fame. But those of the present who use autographs and paintings for their knavery do so only in order to obtain funds for whoring and gambling. They degrade what evinces the splendour of Heaven to the squalor of Hell. Like malicious goblins grabbing what they can by their mean tricks they are often successful—but in the end they will suffer hunger and cold. Why is this so? Because forgers have a fundamental flaw in their character. Lacking a moral basis, how

---

* Chinese: *li-te, li-kung, li-yen* "establish virtue, merit and words"—the three imperishable qualities of a man; quoted from *Tso-chuan*, the 24th year of Duke Hsiang.

could they establish themselves? With them it is easy come easy go, and exactly like common thieves they end their days in misery."

* * *

The perusal of Lu Shih-hua's Scrapbook—and indeed of any other old or later critical Chinese treatise on the connoisseurship of pictorial art—will leave the present-day collector in rather a perturbed state of mind. He will ask himself: If Chinese experts of former times had already so much difficulty in acquiring genuine old paintings, what about my own collection? How can I know whether they are not copies or fakes?

The answer is quite simple: you can't. At least not at the present stage of Chinese art-criticism. The best one can do now is to verify whether an antique painting or autograph dates approximately from the period of the artist whose name it bears, and whether the style approaches in a reasonable degree that artist's brush-technique. But whether it was actually painted or written by him can not be decided—not even in the case of those scrolls the antecedents of which are known several centuries back, such as for instance some items in the Old Palace Collection in Peking, or in some old Japanese collections. Generally speaking the chances that a scroll is genuine, or at least a good contemporary copy, are better when it is signed by a lesser known and later artist, and worse in the case of a famous old master.

The best recommendation I can give to fellow-collectors is to adopt the only criterium that, during more than twenty years of collecting, I have never found to fail me, and that is: whether you really like a picture. If you purchase a painting or autograph that really appeals to you, you can never go wrong. If after further study it should prove to be a copy or a paraphrase, or even a forgery, that should not affect its esthetic value for you. And if it should prove to be perfectly genuine, so much the better! This reduces the problem to the question whether you really know what you like. And as with most problems this bewildering human existence confronts us with, the final answer also to this one lies within ourselves rather than outside.

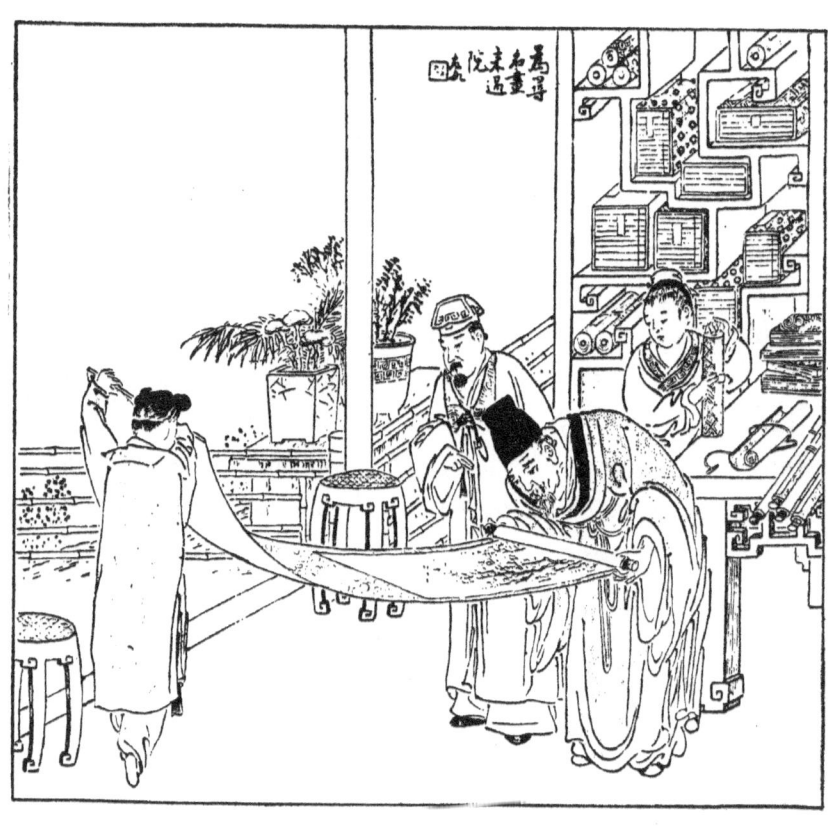

Showing a scroll picture to a friend.
From the Wu-ju-yu-hua-pao, a collection of reproductions of paintings by Wu Yu, an artist who worked in Shanghai ca. 1880.

SCRAPBOOK FOR CHINESE COLLECTORS
PREFACE

Ever since the Han period, our art of letters has been flourishing, and literary compositions show great variety in form. Next to proclamations, memorials, verses, poetical essays, poems, elegies, songs, hymns, epitaphs, biographies, tomb inscriptions, manifests, prefaces, annals, obituaries, official notes and private letters, there is also a form of literature called "sayings," *shuo*. Discussions of the truth of Reason (*li*) and the equipoise of the Way (*tao*), are called "orthodox sayings," those elucidating the Classics and interpreting history are called "commentaries," or also "explanatory sayings." Literary works that broach subjects the ancients did not yet discuss are called "original," those that repeat what others have already said are called "plagiarism." Books broadly discoursing on past and present affairs are called "miscellaneous sayings," and collections of the common talk of the street are called "vulgar sayings," or also "small talk"—that is novels. And books on corrupt studies and heterodox doctrines are called "false sayings."

Now calligraphy and painting are skills, but they embody the Great Way. Calligraphy originated from the drawing of the Eight Triagrams (1), and thence developed the great and small seal, chancery, regular, running and cursive writing, each of these six scripts having its own type and its own standards. Taking rightness as yardstick, one can say that if the heart of the writer is right, his handwriting will also be right. That one statement sums up calligraphy.

As regards painting, this art started with people copying mountains, dragons, water plants and flames (2), and thence developed into the painting of images of saints and sages, of gods and Buddhist deities. Landscapes, flowers and fruit, birds and quadrupeds, all these subjects developed their own style, and of each a special school came into being. But the essence of all pictures lies in their faithfully transmitting the artist's soul (3).

The documentation of artistic matters necessarily has a long history, the people of former generations have treated the subject exhaustively, so that there is no need for us to discuss or elucidate. But although one can say nothing quite original about this subject, that should be no reason to resort to plagiarism. Those who do not know pictorial art should not speak about the corrupt practices connected with it. But there are things one can hardly bear to say, and yet can not leave unsaid; such as the utilizing of autographs and pictures for financial gain, and the production of forgeries: one begins by deceiving strangers, and ends up with deceiving one's friends, nay even one's father, brother, and teacher—and all that without being in the least ashamed. That sufficiently shows the bent of mind of the vulgar crowd.

Some of those abuses, some of that idle gossip, I place here on record, weeping in sadness; for these are not the kind of things one can talk about leisurely and unconcernedly. Although I could not avoid describing trifling and vulgar matters, I am at least certain that my words shall not be called "false sayings."

— I —

The philosopher Hsün Yüeh (4) has said: "Good and evil must be assessed by the resulting merit and sin, one should not wantonly blame and praise. Listening to people's words one must tax them with their actions, relevating their reputation one must point to their deeds. If their performance does not come up to their reputation, then this is called *vain*. If their feelings do not correspond to their outer appearance, then this is called *hypocrisy*. If blame and praise miss the truth, then this is called *false*. And if words and deeds are not analogous, then this is called *deceit*."

With regard to current affairs of the present day one can not hope that there will be no vanity and hypocrisy, and no falsehood and deceit (5). This also applies to smaller matters such as autographs and paintings which emanate from the ancients. The ancients are gone, one can not raise them from the Nether World to question them. Since thus one cannot arrive at the truth without making vain and deceptive statements, why should one wrangle noisily about it?

Since one cannot arrive at the truth in the affairs of the Empire without getting involved in vanity, hypocrisy, falsehood and deceit, for the time being I concentrated on achieving this aim with regard to pictures and autographs. But the affairs of the Empire depend on the abilities of the people of the Empire. How could a poor and lowly student like I, without much prestige and with very limited opportunities, ever hope to be able to impart knowledge about artistic matters? From olden times till the present, forgers of scrolls have displayed rare skill. This I have done my utmost to investigate, hoping that at least in this one minor aspect I have arrived at the truth and done away with vanity and deceit, pointing out right and wrong and establishing black and white.

— II —

The pictures and autographs recorded in my catalogue are of a slightly different kind as those listed by former collectors. Those would immediately enter in their catalogues famous scrolls handed down from one generation to another, renowned items which fetch high prices. Minor or incomplete items they did not bother about. But I pay ever more attention to fragmentary and incomplete scrolls. I was born in this late age, and famous scrolls are now rarely seen. Moreover, I have no social relations with prominent persons. The scrolls I see are what was left over when old families were broken up, the treasured possessions of hermit priests and poor scholars. And why should not these minor items represent the innermost thoughts of the ancients, and harbour their wisdom? Moreover, the famous scrolls that for a long time have been seen and talked about, everyone is familiar with those. But if minor items are not placed on record, I greatly fear that they will be lost for ever.

— III —

Every time I see a picture or an autograph I forthwith make a note of it on a scrap of paper, and throw it in a jar. These notes serve as a record of the works of art I have seen, and also to preserve the ink-remains of eminent writers and painters.

I never attempted to arrange this material into categories and sections, neither did I observe the sequence of the dynasties. Now that I happen to take those notes out and contemplate them, it strikes me that some concern the works by the loyal and the filial, others those of the chaste and righteous; some regard the works of persons who became known by their impartiality and their integrity, or famous as writers and wine bibbers; some regard the works of persons whose passionate disposition involved them into amorous entanglements, or also of people of broad and perspicacious mind who counted riches and honours as floating clouds; others again whose pride drove them to a life in retirement, and others who concentrated on transmitting the Buddhist or Taoist doctrines. All these different personalities are recognizable in the pictures they painted, and in the poems and essays they recorded on their scrolls (6). Therefore, when I now collect these notes in book form, has not that a wider scope than just pictures and autographs?

I still did not adopt a division into categories, but I did arrange the items according to dynasty; but within one dynasty I did not always observe strict chronological order.

— IV —

Autographs and pictures serve our delectation, but their scope is much wider than that alone. The poems and essays recorded on the scrolls may be verified by referring to the published literary works of their writer, landscape pictures may elucidate passages in books on geography (7). Further, the artist's wisdom or folly, his worth or worthlessness, all the strong and weak points in his character often come to light in his brush work. These are extra-acquisitions that accrue from the study of paintings and autographs.

— V —

Persons who while discussing an autograph or a painting expand on generalities in a grandiloquent manner, belong to the lowest category of connoisseurs; among them are those who hope to assert their opinion although they know quite well that the scroll they discuss is a fake. Persons who only hold forth on the price and value of a scroll also belong to the lowest category; among them are those who do not see the implied purpose of the picture, nor where it shows the spirit of its creator.

It is a mistake to value only antique pictures, and despise modern ones. With the passing of time antique scrolls grow less and less. If one insists on collecting only antique pictures one will end up with nothing but fakes.

If one compares painters of the present dynasty like Wang Shih-min (1592-1680 A.D.), Wang Chien (1598-1677 A.D.), Wang Yüan-ch'i (1642-1715 A.D.), Wang Hui (1632-1717 A.D.), Yün Shou-p'ing (1633-1690 A.D.) and Wu Li (1632-1715 A.D.) (8) with the great masters of the Sung and Yüan periods, one shall find that the former exceed rather than fall short of the latter's achievements. And genuine, superior scrolls by those later artists are now already rare—not to speak about the future!

— VI —

In order to judge the authenticity of a famous scroll which is reliably documented, one must verify whether or not it evinces the artist's personality. Thus one may decide whether it is an old copy, or an original work of art.

If the personality is there, and the picture is also of high quality, that means that the artist achieved full self-expression, though modeling his work after the methods of the ancients.

If the personality is there but the picture not beautiful, it means that the artist was too intent, and thus could not rise above his media and his subject.

Pictures lacking both personality and beauty are mere daubs.

Pictures without personality but yet beautiful point to natural talent.

As regards copies, if they are really well done they will resemble the original like two halves of a tally. Clumsy copies do not resemble anything at all. Clever copies where the maker infused something of his own personality are beautiful, provided that there was congenial inspiration and harmony with the mood of the original artist.

There are also pictures that have individuality but still lack style. That means that the artist planned and plodded over his work so intently that he ended up by producing an untrue picture.

A discerning person who grasps the meaning and portent of these principles will apply them ever more expertly to the pictures he sees, and his connoisseurship will improve with every year that passes. But those who run counter to them will stay vague and undecided in their artistic judgement till the end of their days, and even if they do their best it will be of no avail.

— VII —

Sometimes you will hear that an old family possesses a famous scroll. Vexed that you do not know that family, after having tried all kinds of approaches at last you succeed in being admitted to their house. Then, if the owner does not raise any objections but gladly takes out his treasured painting to show it to you; if the scroll not only comes up to your expectations but the owner also does not press you to get over with it in a hurry, if he offers you tea when you are thirsty together with something to eat; and if when you are about to take your leave after having enjoyed the scroll to the full the owner says: "I still have other scrolls which you have not yet seen," and takes out some more pictures, all of rare quality—then this is truly a great joy!

If, on the other hand, when you have heard about a wonderful scroll and go to see it, it proves to be a patent fake; or if, when you visit the owner he raises all kinds of difficulties and invents excuses for not showing you the picture, saying that he has just lent it to a friend, or that he has sold it already, or again that he has offered it as a present to some high official—then this truly is a tremendous nuisance.

— VIII —

The likes and dislikes of people are different. If

I look at famous scrolls together with some one who says: "This one is refined. This one is inspired. And this one is wonderful," everytime saying exactly what was in my own mind, and exactly expressing my own feelings—then this is indeed a great joy!

If, on the other hand, such a person idly chatters away all the time, not only showing that he is absolutely impervious to the beauty that is displayed before him, but on top of that in his talk mixing up the sequence of the dynasties, and while reading out in a loud voice the inscriptions on the scrolls, scanning the text wrongly and making mistakes in the most elementary characters — then this truly is a tremendous nuisance.

— IX —

It may happen that when visiting a curio shop you find a most interesting picture. If because the dealer does not recognize the great artist who painted it, you obtain this scroll for less than half of its real value, then this is truly a great joy. Or, some other time, you may think that the dealer will certainly not realize the wonderful qualities of a picture. Then you find that on the contrary he is perfectly aware of it; you are full of misgivings and think that since the dealer will ask a considerable price you will certainly be unable to purchase that scroll. If, however, upon casually enquiring about the price, you find that it suits you and if then and there the transaction is concluded—then this is truly a great joy!

If, on the other hand, the dealer begins with asking an exorbitant price, calling together a bunch of his friends to corroborate his protestations, and if he makes all kinds of difficulties about consenting to sell the picture; and if, when the deal is finally agreed upon, he branches off on some other argument, stating that he can not sell it if you do not buy some other object at the same time, or that you must pay extra for the brocade cover or the sandalwood box the scroll is kept in, so that in the end your lips are parched and your tongue dry with arguing and you are full of mortification—then this is indeed a tremendous nuisance.

— X —

In the poems or essays written on a famous scroll, or in the critical comments added to it, there will sometimes occur an expression which you do not understand, or you may be unable to identify the writer; you search through all books and records, but all without avail. Then friends will recommend to you a scholar who all agree is a man of wide learning, and you pay him a visit to ask his opinion. But then you find that either he also is at a loss, or tries to force upon you an explanation that you know to be wrong. Thus you think that you must resign yourself to the problem remaining unsolved for ever. Then one day you happen to meet someone and you mention your problem to him, and he says: "This expression is taken from such-and-such a book," or "It is found in such-and-such literary collection of such-and-such a date," and taking the book referred to shows you that he is right, so that the entire problem becomes perfectly clear to you. If a matter of doubt of several years standing is thus suddenly solved—then this truly is a great joy!

Often when a low-minded person obtains a great scroll, he will not recognize it as such; thinking that the artist was some unknown person, he fears that he will not be able to sell the scroll at a high price. Then he will cut off the original signature, and instead write on the scroll some famous name. Or, annoyed that a scroll has no colophon, he will write on the paper or silk of the picture itself a few spurious appreciative comments. Such things are indeed a tremendous nuisance and such persons deserve to be condemned to the deepest Hell!

— XI —

Sometimes you obtain a famous painting that lacks its original colophon, or you find a genuine colophon without the picture it belongs to. You will then be greatly distressed and sigh over a beautiful thing being thus impaired. Then, some day one of your friends comes to visit you and says: "I happened to acquire this picture which unfortunately is incomplete. Allow me to present it to you!" If when he shows it to you it turns out to be the very thing you were looking for to complete your scroll, and when thus "the two swords of Yen-p'ing are happily reunited" (9)—then this is truly a great joy!

On the other hand, a genuine specimen of great beauty may have a faked colophon attached to it, while the real colophon has been attached to a faked scroll. Both are brought on the market as a clever stratagem by mean persons who hope thus to make a profit—the genuine picture keeping its value notwithstanding the faked colophon, and the faked scroll becoming more vendable because of the genuine colophon. If when in due course you learn that one of these two items has been sold to this person and the other to some one else, and if then neither of the two is willing to part with his purchase so that this work of art will never become complete again—then this is truly a tremendous nuisance!

— XII —

Those who compiled catalogues of pictures and autographs either only recorded the names of the artists and the number of their works, or they recorded also the inscriptions and signatures found on each item. Beginning with the *Hsüan-ho-shu-hua-pu* there appeared in succession the *Hua-chi*, the *Wang-shih-shu-hua-yüan*, the *Shu-hua-lu*, the *T'ieh-wang-shan-hu* by Chu Ts'un-li, the *T'ieh-wang-shan-hu* by Tu Mu, the *Ch'ing-ho-shu-hua-fang*, the *Pao-hui-lu*, the *Chen-chi-jih-lu*, the *T'u-hui-pao-chien*, the *Wu-sheng-shih-shih*, the *Ku-chin-fa-shu*, the *Ming-hua-t'i-po*, the *Shan-hu-wang* by Wang K'o-yü, the *Shu-hua-t'i-po-chi* by Yü Feng-ch'ing, the *Hsiao-hsia-chi* by Ch'en Wu-t'ing, and the *Hsiao-hsia-lu* by Kao Shih-ch'i (10). The autographs and paintings listed in the last catalogue are all so famous that they dazzle our eyes!

Once a friend seeing me collect incomplete pictures and fragments of autographs derided me. But I said: "Why should you consider my labour as lowly? How would I attempt to vie with the great collectors? I do this just for my own enjoyment!"

High metropolitan officials have sufficient influence and money to obtain costly scrolls, and they have moreover regular social intercourse with famous men and exalted persons, so that they can see even more rare items. And although for instance Chu Ts'un-li mentioned here above was a poor scholar, he lived in the Hung-chih (1488-1505 A.D.) and Cheng-te (1506-1521 A.D.) periods, when there were still possibilities of good old pictures coming into the hands of common people. Moreover, among the persons he associated with there were men like Shen Chou (1427-1509 A.D.) and Wen Cheng-ming (1470-1559 A.D.) and his sons Wen P'eng (1498-1573 A.D.) and Wen Chia (1500-1582 A.D.)—all famous connoisseurs of that age (11) who were experts in choosing good items. Thus Chu can be compared with the poor wretch who visited the Palace of the Dragon King (12) underseas and saw there the rarest treasures.

But I live in an age where all good antique paintings and autographs have already been searched out, and also I am lacking sympathetic friends. Although since more than twenty years I have given up all hope of becoming famous or wealthy, I collect pictures and autographs to while away the months and years. Up to the present I have been roaming along the deserted banks of lonely watercourses for more than thirty years, and I only saw these few scrolls recorded in my catalogue. I was born in the wrong time and in the wrong place, it is not because my knowledge and apperception are inferior to those of the great collectors of former ages mentioned above.

— XIII —

If one insists on having only things of perfect beauty, one shall certainly excite the ire of Creative Nature (13). And if one insists on collecting only things of great rarity, one shall certainly end up with nothing but fakes. And this applies not only to pictures and autographs, but also to all other antiques.

My late grandfather the Imperial Censor, and my late father the Honorary Secretary (14), lived both during the early half of the K'ang-hsi period. Together with such eminent statesmen as Han T'an (15), Wu Ching (16), T'ang Yu-tseng (17) and Ho Ch'o (18), they devoted themselves to the study of administrative affairs, yet always took pleasure in the collecting of scrolls and other antiques. Everytime when they had obtained one or two lines of a Sung rubbing of a famous autograph, they would greatly treasure such a fragment and did not worry about acquiring the rest of the document. For as soon as one has come to know the brush technique and the spirit of the work of the ancient artists, one can derive the rest by analogy, according to the traditional spirit of the Hsiao Library (19). One fragment of old jade, one piece of old bronze—these suffice by themselves to show the spirit of high antiquity. They would fondle it incessantly and could not bear to let it leave their hands. They would study what piece such a fragment had formed part of, and in what time it had been made. The gentlemen-scholars of old cared about the study of antiques, they never cared about gaining material profit by them.

However, present-day people want jades of the three ancient dynasties Hsia, Shang and Chou only, and then their colour must absolutely be purely white, "sweet-yellow" or "sweet-green" (20). Even then they are not satisfied, they insist that the red spots are spread evenly over its entire surface, and moreover want the object to be large, and in perfect condition. If one sets his standard as high as all that, one had better have a jade object newly made, and submit it to the oil treatment!

If when collecting bronzes of the three antique dynasties one insists on having tripods of the Hsia and vases of the Shang period, and then only those that have a patina showing all the five colours, distinct and clear, and also demanding that the object be completely undamaged—then one had better have new bronzes cast and "age" them by the burning process! (21).

And as regards porcelain, if one insists on having nothing but Ch'ai, Ju, Kuan and Ko wares, and of those only flower vases and incense burners, all of the right enamel and gloss—then one had better travel to Kiangsi Province and have new vessels made after the antique models, and dull their gloss by rubbing them with sand, grindstone and paste! (22).

Finally, if with regard to paintings and autographs one limits his interest strictly to specimens from the Chin, T'ang, Sung and Yüan dynasties, and then only those whose paper is still white (23) or whose silk is in perfect condition—then one had better take up one's brush and paint them himself! For there is no other way about it.

— XIV —

Collector's seals (24) should not be stamped arbitrarily on a painting or autograph, for these seals have their fixed places. In some cases you should use a large seal, in others a smaller one; sometimes seals with red legends, at others seals with white legends. And if there should be no suitable place left on a scroll, then you had better leave it without your seals.

Poems and colophons should not be added arbitrarily either. Every poem has its own meaning, every colophon should uncover a special point connected with the picture. The size of the characters, their style—all such features should be decided upon in accordance with the picture. However, one sees often that people just jot down a few meaningless sentences on a scroll. Why is this necessary? One should not behave like a first-grade student who at the triennial examinations must arrive punctually. Nearly all people of the Ming dynasty indulged continually in this bad habit, not to speak of present-day people! I for one do not presume on my own capacities, when asked to write something on a scroll for others I immediately do so, but always on a separate strip of paper so that afterwards people can retain it or throw it away.

— XV —

The picture "Peach Blossoms and Mountain Birds" by the Yüan artist Chang Shou-chung (25) is a famous painting, listed in Kao Shih-ch'i's *Hsiao-hsia-lu*. Recently it passed into the hands of a certain person in Soochow who greatly loved it and kept it carefully locked away.

Now the most cunning and unscrupulous mounter in Soochow knew a certain official in the district who when visiting the atelier of the mounter would always expatiate on the merits of Chang Shou-chung's picture. Therefore the mounter went to visit the owner and remarked that in the course of the years the paste used for the mounting of the painting had lost its force and that thus its paper had developed wrinkles; he added that the constant rolling and unrolling was liable to cause damage to the painting, and that it should be remounted with very thin paste, then it could be preserved without deteriorating further. The owner believed these words and entrusted the scroll to him.

The mounter then hired an expert and had him make an exact copy of the picture. One day, when the mounter expected a visit of the official, he displayed the original picture that he was remounting on a pasting-board hung high on the wall. The official came indeed and asked: "Why did the owner bring out this scroll?" The mounter asnwered: "Having enjoyed it so long, he became tired of it. He wants to have it remounted and then intends to sell it for the same price he bought it for." The official said: "I know what the original price was, and I want to buy it." The mounter said: "But must I then go without any profit?" The official answered: "I shall certainly give you a suitable reward," and he went home to fetch the money.

The mounter then put the copy up on the board instead of the original. Shortly afterwards the official came back and handed to the mounter the price of the scroll together with an extra reward. The mounter expressly sent some one to fetch a servant of the owner of the scroll whom he had taken into his plot. The servant received the price of the scroll which later he gave to the mounter, he himself keeping the reward. The mounter nicely remounted the copy and handed it over to the official. The original was returned to the owner and there the matter ended. Later the official realized that he had been deceived, but then nothing more could be done about it.

— XVI —

Recently there was an expert in the manufacture of fakes. Another man whom we shall call Liu (26) invested several ounces of silver in this undertaking and ordered him to produce all kinds of faked pictures, which he had mounted in a hurry. But everyone detected in them the forger's technique, so that his patron had no means of disposing of the forgeries.

Now at present those persons who purchase antiques on behalf of high officials are called "buying agents." Among those there was one who lacked both the necessary knowledge and the discerning eye, and Liu thought of selling him the collection of fakes. But he feared that the agent would employ the service of a connoisseur who would recognize the scrolls as fakes.

In Soochow there was a pawnshop that occasionally would accept autographs and paintings. Liu went there and took one of the clerks in his plot. He deposited the entire collection of forgeries there, and took out a back-dated pawn ticket, without receiving any money. Liu went with this pawn ticket to the ignorant agent and said: "You know that I have a large collection of antiques, and that I cannot keep all of them. You also know that that pawnshop often declares pawned goods forfeited and does not deliver them up. Now all my pictures are in that pawnshop, who knows when I shall be able to redeem them? If you, a gentleman of such excellent taste, are interested, I have here the pawn ticket." The ignoramus then said: "I shall redeem the scrolls, paying the original sum you received plus the interest. If the scrolls are good, I shall settle the balance with you, if not then I shall keep them." Liu said: "All right, as you wish!" The agent redeemed the paintings and thus fell into the trap.

— XVII —

I have a friend who is very fond of autographs, paintings and other antiques; he had an extensive collection, genuine and false in about equal portions. But he often exchanged his antiques for those of other people (27), who took them away and brought them back as they liked. Thus very soon he had nothing but fakes!

Another friend of mine uses to buy objects for his collection, and then again sell them; often also he buys back again what he had sold. After some time he found his money all gone, and his house full of antiques; but those were of a kind that could never be sold again!

— XVIII —

I have heard that a man whom we shall call Wang (28) once went to a curio shop while drunk, and with much money on him. The dealer who had taken in the situation saw Wang pick up a fake jade ring from a tray and fondle it. He knew by Wang's mien that he thought it was real jade. By talking glibly the dealer succeeded in making Wang take out his money and purchase the ring. When Wang had returned home and sobered up he understood that he had been cheated; but for the time being he kept his peace.

Half a year later, a few days before the Dragon Boat Festival (29), Wang went back to that shop accompanied by a man from Shansi Province. They showed the dealer a picture of the devil-queller Chung K'uei, and asked him whether he would take it on commission, to be sold for twenty ounces of silver. The dealer said: "I can hardly accept this picture, it is worth only two ounces. How could I ever sell it for twenty?" Wang said: "This man is from Shansi, he does not know anything about pictorial art. Since now is the time of the festival, why not display this painting for a few days in your shop, and then return it?" The dealer agreed, and hung the painting on the wall.

Then Wang told another man from Shansi Province to frequent that curio shop. When that man saw the painting he exclaimed: "That is a work by a famous artist of our Province! I want to buy it!" The dealer then asked fifty ounces for it. The man said he would pay ten, and finally raised his offer to sixteen. When he was about to leave the dealer said: "This painting I have on commission, I shall have to consult the owner." The man deposited some silver as earnest-money and departed.

The next day Wang and the man who had given the picture on commission came to the shop, and wanted it back. After much hemming and hawing the dealer said: "I have a customer who is willing to pay three ounces for it. You had better sell it!" The man from Shansi laughed loudly and said: "This is a family treasure handed down for several generations! The other day I thought of selling it, only because I lacked money for my traveling expenses. But now I have the necessary funds!" Wang urged his friend several times to sell it, arguing that since he would get a good price for it, why worry about the picture. Finally they made a deal at twelve ounces of silver.

The dealer said he would pay the money the next day, after he would have sold the picture, but the man said: "I am about to board my ship, twenty people are waiting for me! I had better take the painting back." The dealer, reflecting that there was a profit of four ounces in it for him, finally agreed and paid. Thus Wang got back the money paid for the fake jade, with something to spare!

— XIX —

There were two friends, whom we shall call Chang and Li (30). Chang was a good calligrapher and knew about literature, he earned his living dealing in pictures and autographs. Outwardly he looked like a stupid fellow, but he had a mean and tricky disposition. Li was learning from him how to judge antique scrolls, hoping some day also to enter that trade.

After some time Chang said to him: "You have made great progress in connoisseurship!", and made Li buy a scroll which Chang sold for him at a good profit.

Now Li was really a pharmacist, but this success encouraged him to neglect his drug business, and to devote all his efforts to the dealing in antique scrolls. Everytime Li was going to buy a scroll, he would first show it to Chang. If Chang said: "Buy it!" he would buy it, and when Chang said "Leave it!" he would do so too. And if Chang advised him to buy a scroll from him, Li would obediently do so, just like in ancient times Ch'en Hsiang blindly followed Hsü Hsing (31).

After the lapse of some time Li's pharmacy had gone down, and his capital was exhausted. His house was full of pictures and autographs, but no one showed any interest in buying them. He took his collection on an extensive trip, but came back without having sold a single one. When he consulted Chang about his predicament, Chang said: "In this business you must wait for the right time and the right price. Why are you in such a hurry?" But Li's capital had been invested entirely in his scrolls, and the money he owed the retail dealer who supplied his stock of drugs had also been used for buying scrolls. The dealer could not wait any longer, he pressed Li ever more insistently for payment. Li wanted to give him some of his paintings in lieu of cash, but the dealer considered those as so much rubbish and would have spat on them. Since Li had nothing else to offer, the dealer lodged a complaint with the authorities. Li was condemned to a flogging and put in jail. Later Li agreed to sell his house, the dealer had to accept the proceeds as compensation, and there the matter ended. All who heard about this sighed deeply.

Recently I went to a place where all the curio dealers are wont to gather. Chang was there also, grandly holding forth on his skill in making money. I remonstrated with him saying: "Have you recently seen Li? How is he doing?" Chang replied: "That fellow is just a destitute vagabond!" All present burst out laughing. When Chang had left I said: "Let me tell you people a funny story! Once a man walking along the road saw a piece of chewed-out sugar cane. He picked it up, put it in his mouth and chewed it vigorously, but could not get one drop of juice from it. He spat it out and shouted: 'The impudent rascal! To suck it dry like that!' Is this not the same as Chang reviling Li?"

— XX —

While roaming through the district of rivers and lakes I always diligently sought for the traces left by the people of former times. I ascended steep cliffs and searched the waterside, risking my life just for studying from nearby some half-effaced antique inscription. Everytime when I came upon a heap of waste paper I would turn over every sheet, always hoping to discover some interesting item. Thus I gradually also learned about local customs and became familiar with local conditions. Elegant and refined indeed is the subject of autographs and paintings—but alas, unfortunately it has not a few regrettable aspects, not to speak of other things! The Wu-yüeh region is the hub of all highways, everyday there are numerous encounters of old friends. The curio shops in the cities try by all sorts of means to attract these travelers to do business with. The people who solicit customers are called "brokers," there are more of them then one could count, and nearly all are wholly unreliable. As soon as one of them disappears, *another will take his place.*

Wu-yüeh is a good region for merchants to do business, and also a profitable place for "selling flowers"; the waterways are crowded with the pleasure boats of the prostitutes, and every other house is a wineshop. Those people employ all kinds of clever stratagems and tricks to ensnare customers. As soon as one has one foot in it, one will certainly submerge entirely in this dissipated life.

— XXI —

If a scroll does not bear a signature this should not be considered a shortcoming. Many Sung artists neither signed nor sealed their works, and all pictures done in the Palace on Imperial command lack both seals and signatures. Such masters as for instance Ma Yüan and Hsia Kuei (32) sometimes wrote their personal name in very small regular characters in an empty space among the trees or rocks of their pictures, in a lower corner. And Li Lung-mien although he was an expert calligrapher did not like to append his signature to his works. But present-day people when they obtain a genuine painting by him, always will add in a corner the five characters "Li Kung-lin, called Lung-mien." This is an unspeakable sin!

The ancient masters achieved immortality both by their calligraphy and their painting. The art of those men must have been rooted in previous existences, they are born from the refined spirit of streams and mountains. They added to this natural talent a wide artistic experience, and brought to it the result of assiduous practice. Only in this manner could they reach such perfection.

Every one of those masters has his own peculiar style, even in the work of fathers and sons one notices differences. For instance, the handwriting of the calligrapher Wang Hsien-chih (344-388 A.D.) does not quite resemble that of his father, the celebrated Wang Hsi-chih (321-379 A.D.), each of the two had his own special style (33).

This being so, why should artists sign their work? Good connoisseurs will see at a glance that a certain style of brush work must belong to a certain artist. That does not mean that good connoisseurs have supernatural perspicacity. It only means that a given artist's work can never be achieved in quite that way by another, and knowing this connoisseurs will not make mistakes. Each work by an artist represents the results of painstaking labour, how could it not faithfully express his spirit?

Artists who do not sign their work also say often: "The later people must know that only I can have painted this!"—but by "later people" they do not mean superficial and flippant persons. Every generation produces but one or two really great masters, and also only one or two great connoisseurs. Moreover, the latter must also be able to paint and write themselves. T'ang connoisseurs like Ou-yang Hsün (557-641 A.D.), Yü Shih-nan (558-638 A.D.), Ch'u Sui-liang (596-658 A.D.), and Hsüeh Chi (649-713 A.D.) (34), and Sung connoisseurs like Mi Fu (1051-1107 A.D.) and his son Mi Yu-jen (1086-1165) and Su Shih (1036-1101) and his son Su Kuo (1072-1123 A.D.), and Yüan connoisseurs like Chao Meng-fu (1254-1322 A.D.) and his sons Chao Yung and Chao I, and also K'o Chiu-szu (1290-1343 A.D.) (35)—the names of all these men have been preserved and so have their works. If nowadays people are in doubt about the authorship of a scroll, they engage in idle speculations, the only thing they can rely on is their recognizing a famous name. For those people a signature is indeed necessary.

— XXII —

If the artists of the Sung dynasty signed their work with their personal name, they did not add an impression of their seal. And if they sealed their work, they did not add their signature. This can be verified in the works by the calligrapher Huang T'ing-chien (1045-1105 A.D.) (36), and those by my ancestor, the Duke of Wei-nan (i.e. Lu Yu, 1125-1210 A.D.) (37).

— XXIII —

If you cannot obtain the service of a good mounter for remounting your autographs and paintings, you had better leave them as they are, even if they should be badly damaged. You should wrap them up well and keep them in a box, putting no heavy articles on top of them. You should not be in a hurry and entrust such scrolls to a clumsy mounter, for giving a scroll to a clumsy mounter is tantamount to destroying it. It is not for nothing that clumsy mounters are referred to as "Executioners of scrolls."

On the other hand, present-day mounters in Soochow like Chang Yü-jui who is an expert in repairing antique paper scrolls, and Shen Ying-wen who is an expert in repairing antique silk scrolls—these two surpass in their art the mounters of old, and the future shall not produce their equals. They may be compared to famous sages and meritorious statesmen!

— XXIV —

There exist no fixed measurements for autographs and pictures. Everytime the ancient masters happened to obtain a sheet of good paper, they would feel inspired and write or paint on it. At present the size most commonly used is not higher than two feet, and measuring eight or nine inches in breadth.

If curio dealers find an old painting they have no particular use for, they will cut it down so as to remove the signature, and then write on it the name of some famous Sung or Yüan artist instead. They go even so far as to cut up a very large painting into three or four smaller ones, and write on each of those auspicious titles. When they have in this way assembled a hundred or so of such cut-up paintings, they go and sell them in another locality.

At first I thought that those people engaged in a very risky undertaking indeed. But after a few months I saw them come back with money, or with merchandise they had bought with the money earned with their forgeries; the goods they sold in their home village, and with the money they purchased some small official rank for themselves. When I asked them about this they said: "The value of the name of a Sung or Yüan artist ranges within several ounces gold; thus each of those faked scrolls will make us gain several times our original outlay!" This is something I would never have suspected.

— XXV —

If you lock your autographs and paintings carefully away, never showing them to others, and even yourself never looking at them, this is like burying a great treasure in a deep well, and a wholly irrational attitude. On the other hand, however, you should neither be too liberal in showing your treasures. If your guest has not the slightest understanding for pictorial art, and only listlessly unrolls and rolls the pictures, even touching them with greasy fingers or moistening them with spittle while talking, this only brings harm and no gain.

— XXVI —

The conservation of famous scrolls depends entirely upon the way they are stored away. If you put them in a place where they are eaten by insects or gnawed at by rats, then this is an even greater sin than throwing good rice among dirt.

— XXVII —

Autographs and paintings should be displayed in proper surroundings. A beautiful landscape garden is a most appropriate place for viewing scrolls. Or also the rustic pleasaunce or the thatched hut of a retired scholar, if swept clean and tidy, will always provide the right atmosphere.

Spacious halls and luxurious courts will by their dazzling splendour detract from the beauty of the pictures shown there. If one suspends there a fine painting in the middle, hanging on either side red scrolls or antithetical couplets written in vulgar script, the text of which refers to official honours and signed by persons of influence and authority; or if one places on the table underneath artificially-aged bronze vessels, fans of peacock feathers or foreign-made striking clocks—then this is grievous company for a scroll (38).

— XXVIII —

It is difficult to give a definite lead for the judging of antique scrolls. If one is suddenly confronted with a good copy of a work by an artist whose originals one has not yet seen, one will yet have his suspicions, just as if one were familiar with that artist's style. Thus a good connoisseur will at least not commit gross errors —like "mistaking a deer for a horse." But one cannot expect this of persons who lack the necessary knowledge and the discerning eye (39).

— XXIX —

Do not discuss authenticity problems with outsiders, that is a mere waste of lips and tongue. Every item they discuss means for you an additional bother, the less they say the better. And for your own peace of mind you had better remain silent too. If not, the vulgar atmosphere will become insupportable!

Written in the sixth moon of the year 1776, by the "Mountain Recluse listening to the Pines," when he found himself at leisure while fleeing the summer heat.

NOTES

(1) Eight Triagrams. These are the basis of the *I-ching*, the ancient Book of Divination, and they are traditionally considered to be the origin of Chinese writing. The reader is referred to the excellent account by W.R.B. Acker, page 85 sq. of his book *Some T'ang and pre-T'ang texts on Chinese painting*, Sinica Leidensia vol. VIII, Leiden 1954.

(2) Mountains, dragons etc. Quoted from the *Shu-ching*, the ancient Book of Documents, chapter Kao-yao-mo, section 12, where the Emperor says: "I desire to contemplate the symbols of the ancients, sun, moon, stars, *mountains*, *dragons*, and flowery animals, as are depicted on sacrificial vessels; and *water plants*, *flames*, grain, rice etc. as embroidered on garments." According to an age-old tradition all treatises on pictorial art should begin with a similar passage where the origin of calligraphy and painting is projected into mythical antiquity.

"If the heart is right, the handwriting will also be right." This is an often-quoted pronouncement by the T'ang calligrapher Liu Kung-ch'üan (778-865 A.D.) who was famous as an expert in *kai-shu*, the regular script.

(3) "Soul resonance," *shen-yün*; cf. the explanation of this term on page XXXI of Acker's book quoted above.

(4) Hsün Yüeh (148-209 A.D.) was a Han writer known for his excellent style. Since I do not have his works at hand here, I am unable to check the context of the passage quoted; my translation is based on Lu Shih-hua's interpretation.

(5) This chapter contains two phrases that apparently gave offense to the Ch'ing censors and caused the entire book to be

placed on the Index. The first line of the second paragraph implies criticism of the government, and the first line of the third paragraph can be read in an anti-dynastic sense. I translated: "Since one can not arrive at the truth in the affairs of the Empire without getting involved in vanity, hypocrisy, falsehood and deceit, for the time being I concentrate on achieving this aim with regard to pictures and autographs." In the Chinese text "to arrive at the truth" reads *kuei yü chen-shih*, literally: "to return to truth." Now *kuei* means especially "to return something where it truly belongs." Thus the phrase could—and evidently was meant to—be interpreted also as meaning: "Since now the Empire cannot be given back to its true owner, i.e. the Ming Imperial House, for the time being I can do no better than to confine myself to artistic matters, trying to arrive at the truth at least in this one minor subject."

— III —

(6) This chapter shows clearly that whereas we are wont to consider a work of art entirely on its own merits, Chinese critics attach great importance to the degree in which such a work expresses the personality of the artist. This consideration influences their appraisal as much as the intrinsic artistic qualities.

— IV —

(7) Here again we notice an important difference in the attitude of Chinese art-critics, this time caused by the preponderant role played by literary studies, also in the field of fine art. For the Chinese connoisseur the documentary value of a picture is an important criterium when appraising its quality.

— V —

(8) The six painters mentioned are considered the greatest artists in traditional style of the Ch'ing period, excelling especially

in landscapes. Cf. V. Contag, *Die sechs berühmten Maler der Ch'ing Dynastie* (1 vol., Leipzig 1940), where life and works of these six masters are discussed in detail.

— XI —

(9) "The two swords of Yen-p'ing," allusion to a story told about the famous Chin writer Chang Hua (232-300 A.D., author of the *Po-wu-chih*), and his friend Lei Huan. The latter discovered a pair of antique swords, respectively called Lung-ch'üan and T'ai-ngo; one he kept himself, the other he presented to Chang. After Chang's death, the sword Lei had given to him unaccountably disappeared. When Lei had also died, his son once visited Nan-p'ing (in Fukien Province) where Chang had lived and, carrying his father's sword, passed by the Yen-p'ing Ford nearby. Suddenly the sword jumped from its sheath and into the water. Then two dragons were seen sporting together in the waves; it were the souls of the sword-pair, now happily re-united. The text has *Yen-chin,* short for Yen-*p'ing*-chin. The full story is found in Chang Hua's biography in ch. 105 of the *Chin-shu*, "History of the Chin Dynasty."

In China there exists an extensive sword-lore, every famous blade has its own individual name, and many tales are told about their magic properties. *Shuang-chien*, "pairs of swords" are used in two-handed fencing, their length and weight are carefully adjusted to each other, hence such a pair should never be separated; such pairs are also referred to as *tz'u-hsiung-chien* or *yin-yang-chien*, "female and male." Swords and dragons are closely connected; sword-lore abounds in stories about swords changing into dragons, and vice-versa.

— XII —

(10) Nearly all the 17 works enumerated here are well-known handbooks; the list is interesting in so far that it shows

NOTES 73

which of the numerous books of this kind an 18th century connoisseur had on his shelves. Here follow some details of each item :

Hsüan-ho-shu-hua-pu, catalogue of autographs and paintings in the Palace Collection during the reign of the Sung Emperor Hui-tsung.

Hua-chi, a work on pictorial art in 10 ch., by the Sung scholar Teng Chun.

Wang-shih-shu-hua-yüan, a large collection of older works on pictorial art, collected by the Ming scholar Wang Shih-chen (1526-1590 A.D.).

Shu-hua-lu, apparently an abbreviated title; there are many works the title of which ends with these three words "Records of autographs and paintings."

T'ieh-wang-shan-hu (shu-hua-p'in), a catalogue in 16 ch. compiled by the Ming bibliophile and connoisseur Chu Ts'un-li (1444-1513 A.D.); the text gives his style Hsing-fu. Only about 70 antique scrolls are described, but all of those are well-known items.

T'ieh-wang-shan-hu, a catalogue in 20 ch., published by the Ming collector and painter Tu Mu who flourished ca. 1500; the text gives his literary name Nan-hao. He published several other books on pictorial art.

Ch'ing-ho-shu-hua-fang, 12 ch., catalogue of paintings from the Period of the Three Kingdoms till ca. the middle of the Ming dynasty. Compiled by the connoisseur and landscape painter Chang Ch'ou (original name Ch'ien-te), whose preface is dated 1616.

Pao-hui-lu, a catalogue in 20 ch. of scrolls collected by the Ming connoisseur Chang T'ai-chieh, whose preface is dated 1633.

Chen-chi-jih-lu, in 5 ch., with two sequels each of 1 ch.; a catalogue of famous scrolls seen by Chang Ch'ou, mentioned above.

T'u-hui-pao-chien, 5 ch., a history of painting from early beginnings till the end of the Yüan dynasty, compiled by the connoisseur Hsia Wen-yen, whose preface is dated 1365; the Ming scholar Han Ang added a sequel which brings the contents up to ca. 1500 A.D.

Wu-sheng-shih-shih, a catalogue of Ming paintings in 7 ch., compiled by the Ch'ing connoisseur Chiang Shao-shu.

Ku-chin-fa-shu "Model autographs of old and modern times." May refer to several works of this genre.

Ming-hua-t'i-po "Superscriptions and colophons of famous paintings," unidentified.

Shan-hu-wang, a comprehensive collection, in 48 ch., of extracts from older works on pictorial art, 24 ch. on calligraphy and 24 on painting. Edited by the Ming scholar Wang K'o-yü 1587-ca. 1650 A.D.). In 1936 the Commercial Press in Shanghai published a reprint in 2 foreign volumes.

Shu-hua-t'i-po-chi, 12 ch., a collection of notes on antique scrolls, publ. by the Ming connoisseur Yü Feng-ch'ing.

Hsiao-hsia-chi, by Ch'en Wu-t'ing. This book is unknown to me; Wu-t'ing was the literary name of the Ch'ing scholar Ch'en T'ing-ching (1639-1712), but his biography does not say that he wrote this catalogue.

(*Chiang-ts'un*) *hsiao-hsia-lu*, a descriptive catalogue of famous scrolls, in 4 ch., compiled by the scholar-artist Kao Shih-ch'i (1645-1703). Being high in the Emperor's favour he was familiar with the Palace Collection, and had excellent opportunities for seeing also the scrolls in great private collections. This book is generally considered as the standard-catalogue.

NOTES

(11) Shen Chou, in the text referred to by his style Ch'i-nan, was one of the great landscape painters of the Ming period, also known as a calligrapher, poet and essayist. He is considered the teacher of Wen Cheng-ming, who became also famous as a poet, painter and calligrapher. His eldest son Wen P'eng was a well-known scholar-artist who painted landscapes, flowers and plants. Wen Chia, the second son, was a good landscapist but known especially as a connoisseur.

(12) According to Chinese folklore the Dragon King, Lung-wang, lives in a magnificent palace on the bottom of the sea where he has hoarded fabulous treasures. There are many old stories about fishermen, poor students etc. who after many adventures found their way there and were well received by the Dragon King, some even marrying one of the Princesses. Lu Shih-hua uses this allusion to stress the difficulty of getting access to the great collections of antique scrolls.

— XIII —

(13) The belief that too beautiful things or persons excite the envy of the gods is of course quite a common one both East and West.

(14) *Ju-lin*. According to Lu Shih-hua's tomb inscription, his father was a *Ju-lin-lang* "Secretary of the Forest of Literati," a purely honorary rank, of the 6th degree.

(15) Han T'an (1637-1704 A.D.), in the text referred to by his literary name Mu-lu, was a well-known scholar and statesman, who served i.a. as President of the Board of Ceremonies, and Chancellor of the Han-lin Academy.

(16) Wu Ching, referred to by his lit. name Hsi-chai, lived 1662-1707 A.D. and was a poet of note.

(17) T'ang Yu-tseng (lit. name Hsi-ai, 1656-1722 A.D.) was a great scholar, specially known for his poetry.

(18) Ho Ch'o (lit. name I-men, 1661-1722 A.D.) was a famous classical scholar, also known as a collector of rare books and manuscripts.

(19) "Hsiao Library" refers to a story told about the T'ang poet Li Yüeh (flourished ca. 800 A.D.). When he had obtained one, very large character *hsiao* written on the wall of a temple by the famous calligrapher Hsiao Tzu-yün (486-549 A.D.), he built a large hall especially to house this one character, and called it Hsiao-chai. Chinese calligraphers and painters often worked directly on the plaster wall; such autographs or pictures could be removed by carefully peeling off the plaster coating, and placing it in a wooden frame.

(20) "Sweet yellow," *kan-huang* and "sweet green," *kan-ch'ing*, are technical terms employed by jade collectors, and indicate respectively a dark brown and a dark greenish-blue colour. The Chinese distinguish sharply between "antique jade," *ku-yü*, that is found in crude or worked state in China itself, and "new jade" that is imported into China in crude state and subsequently worked. The former is said to be "alive" and "warm," the latter "dead" and "cold." Antique jade is of course considered as much more valuable than new jade, not only because of its value for antiquarian studies but also because it is considered to contain a large supply of "life force" or "virtue," that will communicate itself to him who wears such a piece on his person. The red spots and veins appearing on old jade are likened to blood vessels, pieces showing this feature are highly prized. They are imitated by submitting the piece to a process called *t'i-hung-yu*, i.e. boiling it in oil mixed with certain red pigments, and then polishing it with wax. The reader will find detailed—but not always reliable—

NOTES 77

information on the production of fakes in the small book *Ta-ku-chai-po-wu-hui-chih*, published in Peking in 1919 by a curio-dealer called Ho Ming-chih, interleaved with a French translation, in 2 Chinese volumes. Faked jade is discussed in vol. 2, p. 85 sq.

(21) Chinese forgers employ various methods to give later or newly made bronzes the required antique patina. The method referred to here is called *shao-pan* "produce spots by burning" (also mentioned in Chapter XXVII, and there translated "artificially aged"), and consists in heating the object till it is red-hot, and then covering it with a mixture of resin, alum and clay. This and other methods for faking bronzes are described in Ho Ming-chih's work quoted above, vol. 2, page 38 sq.

(22) In the case of antique lacquer and porcelain the Chinese greatly value a dull shine, technically called *t'ui-kuang* "receded lustre." Forgers imitate this quality by first rubbing the surface of the object with a grindstone, then with a mixture of paste and fine sand, and finally polishing it with a straw pad in order to obliterate the scratches. This same method is regularly used to give cloisonné pieces their finish.

Kiangsi Province has throughout the ages been famous for its kilns.

The four porcelains mentioned are among the finest known, and incense burners and flower vases are most sought after because they can actually be used in the scholar's library. *Ch'ai-yao* is the sky-blue ware of legendary fame, *Ju-yao* is ware produced in Ju-chou, *Kuan-yao* denotes products of the Imperial kilns in Ching-te-chen, and *Ko-yao* is crackled ware.

(23) It will be noticed that in the last passage of this chapter Lu Shih-hua refers to antique scrolls the paper or silk of which have not been toned down by age, as particularly desirable. Chinese collectors attach great importance to that condition, not

only because it shows the scroll in its pristine state, but also because it proves that it was treasured by generations of discerning connoisseurs who were careful never to expose it hanging on the wall for a long time on end. Amateurs, on the contrary, prefer pictures that have acquired an antique tinge, and obliging curio dealers produce this artificially by dyeing the scroll, or exposing it to the smoke of certain oleaginous plants.

— XIV —

(24) Chinese seals are works of art. The legends are carved directly into the seal stone by scholars and calligraphers who express their own style in this "calligraphy with the iron brush." A seal legend is subject to the same rules for balancing and spacing as govern a painting or autograph, and good seals are valued as highly.

Collectors have one or more special seals for impressing on their scrolls to mark them as their property. Antique pictures often show scores of such seals, which may be a great help in establishing their antecedents. For the Chinese eye, those seal impressions do not interfere with the beauty of a picture—provided of course that their place is chosen with care, in harmony with spacing and brushwork of the picture.

Many collectors use preferably a seal carved in relief, so that it leaves an impression where the characters appear in red lines on a white ground; such seals can be impressed on a scroll without obliterating parts of the brushwork. On the other hand, however, a seal carved in intaglio which leaves an impression where the legend appears in white strokes on a red ground, may also do very well if stamped for instance in a corner of a large blank area in a landscape picture, where it emphasizes as it were the impression of space.

NOTES

Inscriptions should be added with even greater care. Not only their location, but also their content, and the size and the style of the characters, must be in harmony with the atmosphere and the style of the picture.

Western students may at first find that those seals and inscriptions added to an antique scroll by later collectors and connoisseurs interfere with its beauty. It will often help if one imagines that one sees the picture in a mirror, on the glass of which are painted the seals and inscriptions. After one has thus learned to see, as it were, *through* those additions, one will gradually come to see them together with the picture again, both elements enhancing each other's beauty.

— XV —

(25) Chang Shou-chung, styled Tzu-cheng, was a painter of the Yüan period. The *Chiang-ts'un hsiao-hsia-lu* lists in ch. 3 a picture by him entitled *T'ao-hua-ch'un-niao-t'u*, described as an ink-painting on paper; *shan* in our text is apparently a mistake for *ch'un*.

— XVI —

(26) The text refers to the forger's patron throughout as "the man who invested the money." Since this reads awkwardly in English I arbitrarily gave that enterprising gentleman the surname Liu.

The agent thought that he could not go wrong on this bargain, for Chinese pawnbrokers, just like their colleagues in other parts of the world, never take risks and advance on pawned goods less than the actual value. But in this case of fraud the clerk had written on the pawnticket an exorbitant amount. After the agent had redeemed the scrolls, the clerk handed that amount to Liu, deducting of course a substantial commission for his cooperation.

— XVII —

(27) It is an age-old custom among Chinese collectors to exchange their antiques, and in their catalogues one will often find at the end of the description of an item the remark: "Exchanged for such-and-such an object with Mr. So-and-so."

The *Hsün-chih-t'ang-tsa-ch'ao* records the extreme case of the Ming bibliophile Chu Ta-shao who once exchanged even a beautiful and cultured concubine for a rare Sung-print he coveted. When leaving Chu's house she wrote the following poem on the wall:

"Without valid reason you gave up what you treasured,
   And drove me away from my sheltered quarters,
With more ease indeed
   Than formerly people changed their horses.
If later you should meet me again
   You had better not be sorry,
For then you'll find the spring blossoms all scattered,
   And my love gone."

The line about changing horses refers to a note in the *Ch'in-hsiao-chih* by the T'ang writer Chu K'uei, who relates that the scholar Ts'ao Chang (flourished ca. 550 A.D.) once exchanged one of his concubines for a race-horse.

— XVIII —

(28) Here the customer who was cheated is referred to as "the drunk of that day"; in the translation I call him Wang.

(29) The Dragon Boat Festival, also called Tuan-yang, is celebrated on the 5th day of the 5th moon. It is customary to display on that day in one's house various kinds of charms that dispel evil influences, and images of Chung K'uei, the awe-inspiring arch-enemy of all devils and goblins, belong to that category.

— XIX —

(30) In the text the two friends are called A. (*Chia*) and B. (*I*). Since A. and B. remind me of algebra sums which used to cast a dark shadow over my schooldays, I call them in my translation Chang and Li, the two common Chinese surnames often used by Chinese writers in the same sense.

(31) Ch'en Hsiang and Hsü Hsing were philosophers of the Agricultural School of the 4th century B.C., who preached a return to a simple life, even the ruler himself tilling the land with his own hands. Ch'en Hsiang had originally different ideas, but as soon as he had met Hsü Hsing he became his devoted follower and gave up all his own convictions.

— XXI —

(32) Ma Yüan and Hsia Kuei were two great landscapists of the Sung dynasty who flourished ca. 1200 A.D. Li Kung-lin (1040-1106 A.D.) was an artist of universal talent, equally famous as a calligrapher, landscapist, and as a painter of horses and human figures.

(33) Wang Hsi-chih is the paragon of calligraphers (in the text he is referred to by his rank, "Commander of the Right Wing"); already during his life time people paid in gold for a few lines written by him. Also his son Wang Hsien-chih (here referred to as the "Senior Magistrate") enjoyed fame as an outstanding calligrapher. It will perhaps strike many Western readers as curious that Lu Shih-hua takes it for granted that the son of an artist will paint or write in exactly the same style as his father. It must be remembered, however, that according to the Chinese traditional conception of *hsiao*, filial piety, it would be considered insufferable impertinence if a son would not aim at continuing as faithfully as possible the style established by his father.

(34) Ou-yang Hsün, Yü Shih-nan, Ch'u Sui-liang and Hsüeh Chi were all famous calligraphers; the text gives only their surnames.

(35) Mi Fu and his son Mi Yu-jen were both famous as painter, calligrapher and connoisseur. Su Shih, better known as Su Tung-p'o, was one of the greatest scholar-artists of the Sung dynasty; C.D. Legros Clark published several of his essays in English translation under the title *The Prose Poetry of Su Tung-p'o* (Shanghai 1935), and Lin Yü-t'ang published a well-written study entitled *The Gay Genius, the life and times of Su Tung-p'o* (New York 1947). His son Su Kuo was known as a poet and painter. The Yüan scholar-artist Chao Meng-fu is known in the West chiefly as a painter of horses, but in China he is especially famous as a calligrapher and connoisseur of autographs. His eldest son Chao Yung continued his father's tradition as scholar-official, the second son Chao I chose the life of a recluse and specialized in the judging of antique scrolls. K'o Chiu-szu, here referred to by his style Ching-chung, was a great connoisseur who on the orders of the Yüan Emperor Wen (1330-1332 A.D.) sifted the autographs and paintings in the Palace collection; he was himself a well-known painter of monochrome sketches of plum blossoms, bamboo and stones.

— XXII —

(36) Huang T'ing-chien was a great poet and calligrapher of the Sung period, especially famous for his cursive handwriting; the text refers to him by his literary name Shan-ku.

(37) Lu Yu was an eminent Sung poet; Wei-nan-kung was his posthumous name.

— XXVII —

(38) The second paragraph refers especially to hanging scrolls used to decorate the main hall of the house. It is customary

NOTES

to hang against the backwall a larger painting, hence called *t'ang-hua* "hall picture," flanked by one or more pairs of *tui-lien*, i.e. very narrow hanging scrolls inscribed with antithetical couplets. *Tui-lien* written on *red* paper are presented to the owner of the house on birthdays, marriages, promotions and other auspicious occasions; they are supposed to be displayed in the hall only on the day of the feast—but vulgar people will often leave them on the wall, especially if they are signed by high officials or other prominent persons.

Underneath the *t'ang-hua* stands a high, narrow table, where one may display some antiques. The Ming connoisseur Wen Chen-heng (1585-1645) observes in ch. 10 of his *Chang-wu-chih*: "On the table standing against the wall underneath the painting one may place a stone of interesting shape, some flowers in season, a miniature tray-landscape, or similar things. But garish objects like red-lacquer work should be avoided." In general the objects displayed there should harmonize with the painting, but in an inobtrusive manner so as to underline its beauty without diverting the observer's attention.

It may be added that the same principles govern in Japan the arrangement of the hanging scroll and accompanying art objects displayed in the *toko-no-ma*, the niche in the reception room in a Japanese house which has the same function as the backwall of a Chinese hall.

— XXVIII —

(39) Special attention is drawn to the last sentence of this chapter. Both East and West one still finds too many persons who are firmly convinced that they possess a natural talent for judging antique paintings, and hence do not need to make a special study of the subject. "Feeling" does indeed play an important role in

the appraising of antique and later works of art, but only when it has been developed by "the necessary knowledge" and when it is supported by "the discerning eye."

書畫說鈴

婁東陸時化聽松著

仁和許 增邁孫刊

兩漢以來。文字蔚興。其體不一。詔誥疏議。詞賦詩騷。歌頌誌狀。銘表記序。哀誄劄子。書牘之外。又有曰說。辨理之正。論道之中。謂之正說。明經斷史。謂之注說。亦云闡說。前人未及謂之創說。人云亦云謂之剿說。統括古今。謂之雜說。街談巷議。謂之俗說。亦云小說。曲學異端。謂之邪說。書與畫技能也。而大道存焉。書肇於畫卦。而篆籀隸正行草。體格遞殊。工拙自判。說之至正者。心正則筆正。一語定之。畫自山龍藻火。至為聖賢神佛圖象。山水花果鳥獸。各立一法。以自成家。歸於有筆墨神韻。而具書卷氣者。其傳必遠。前人之說已盡。無俟後起之辨論闡注。既不能創。亦不可剿也。不知書畫。無可說書畫之流弊。有欲說而不忍。而仍不能已者。自書畫可易貨利而作偽者出。始而欺人。繼而欺友。至及父兄師長。而無怍色。其世俗居心。尚可問乎。一端之弊。一夕之談。山人出之痛哭流涕。非可以從容揮塵時並觀。雖不免為小說俗說。而究不得謂之邪說。

I　荀悅有言。善惡要於功罪。而不淫於毀譽。聽其言而責其事。舉其名而指其實。故實不應其聲者。謂之虛。情不覆其貌者。謂之僞。毀譽失其眞者。謂之誣。言事失其類者。謂之罔。今世上之事。尙不能冀其虛僞不得設。誣罔不得行。區區書畫。出之古人。古人往矣。不能起九原而問之。又烏能歸於眞實而無虛罔。而斷斷論說之哉。惟不能使天下事歸於眞實。而無虛僞誣罔。而姑務之於書畫也。天下之事。出之於天下之人。一草茅賤士。旣無德位。又鮮時勢。其將何以轉移之哉。書畫自古及今。作僞者亦終有數。盡心力而考之。且以此無關重輕之一端。歸於眞實。絕其虛罔。使是非明而黑白定也。

II　今所錄之書畫。與前人少異。前人以相傳之名蹟。著耀而重價者。則亟登焉。一鱗片甲則棄之。余於斷簡殘編。往往更爲留意。余生也晚。名蹟罕見。又未嘗出入朱門。得見者皆故族散亡之餘。及山僧韋儒之什襲。然何一非古人心思知慮之所在。況久著人耳目者。人已知之。此而不載。甚懼泯焉。

III　凡書畫隨見。卽以片紙記之。置之甕中。以當煙雲過眼。亦留雪鴻泥爪。未嘗分門別類。亦不序朝代後先。今偶出而觀之。有忠孝焉。有節義焉。或以廉潔著。或以文酒豪。或鍾情而綢繆感慨。或曠達而富貴浮雲。或寄傲於隱逸。或傳道於釋玄。見之製圖。見之詩歌。因集爲一編。豈獨書畫云乎。門部仍不分。而分之以朝代先後。一朝之人而中有前有後。不及次焉。

IV 書畫供人之娛玩。而非但供人之娛玩。詞賦可與本人之正集參考。圖繪可合山經水乘發明。且作者之知愚賢不肖。及性情之剛柔高卑。往往流露于筆墨之間。此又從書畫之理。而旁見側出者也。

V 論書畫而鋪張揚厲下乘也。明知其僞以冀壯觀者是也。僅論價值之低昂者下乘也。不究其命意之所在。志趣之所存者。是也。尊古而薄今。非也。世日遠而所存日少。必欲致焉則僞而已矣。國朝畫手如王奉常（時敏）王廉州（鑑）王司農（原祁）王山人（翬）惲布衣（初名格後改壽平）吳處士（歷）。較之宋元大家。有過無不及。眞而佳者。今已罕見。況以後乎。

VI 凡名蹟既信而有徵。於眞之中。辨其著意不著意。是臨摹舊本。抑自出心裁。有著意而精者。心思到而師法古也。有著意而反不佳者。過於矜持而執滯也。

有不著意而不佳者。草草也。有不著意而精者神化也。有臨摹而妙者。若合符節也。有臨摹而拙者。畫虎不成也。有自出心裁而工者。機趣發而興會佳也。有自出心裁而無可取者。作意經營而涉杜撰也。此中意味。慧心人愈引愈長。與年俱進。扞格者畢世糢糊。用心亦無益也。

VII 聞一舊家藏一名蹟。苦不相識。鑽頭覓縫。得至其家。主人欣然絕無難色。出而觀之。所見果如所聞。又不相迫促。渴則有飲。飢則有食。盡情覽畢。謝而退。主人曰。尚有君所未聞者。更出一二種。俱是逸品。眞大快事也。或聞其妙而去。旣見卻是極贋。或登其堂。百般推託。非云出借于外。卽是已經售人。已送達官長者。則又大煞風景。

VIII 人之好惡不同。與人共觀名蹟。其人云此種方是逸品。此是神品。此是妙品。與余意中。一一符合。眞大快事也。或妄論不休。不但不著痛癢。所論朝代以前作後。以後作前。朗誦題辭。無非破句。認識字面。盡屬魯魚。則又大煞風景。

IX 偶至市肆。見一最入賞鑒之物。彼不知作者爲何人。不及半價而得之。眞大快事。或藐視爲市人必不知是物之妙處。及至問之。彼已了了於胸中。余爲之躊躇曰。事不諧矣。彼必索重價。姑再問之。所索之價。竟適符其值。頃刻成交。此一大快事也。或值一索百。呼朋引類。互爲圈套。一肯一不肯。旣成交易。又別生枝節云。尙有一物。要牽聯而售。或錦囊檀匣。另要補價。舌敝脣焦。塵生滿襟。則又大煞風景。

X　名蹟中或詩歌詞賦題跋。其中有字義不解。或不知作者之姓名。搜索羣書。考而不得。咸推某爲博覽。造謁請敎。亦殊茫然。或強爲知而支吾。自料此爲畢生疑案。忽逢一人。偶然道及。曰是出何書。或見於某集某代。取冊證之。歷歷在目。積年疑團。一旦冰釋。此眞一大快事。或一名蹟。鄙者以爲此是小名家。難獲重價。割去其款。另書重名。或憎其無跋。於本身紙素。添一二題辭。此則大煞風景。其人必墮阿鼻地獄。

XI　得一名蹟。或有圖而失跋。或有跋而失圖。中心耿耿。有璧破鴛離之歎。忽來一友云。偶拾一物。惜乎不全。敢以持贈。出而視之。卽是余所缺之物。遂爲延津之劍眞大快事。或一名物本是全美眞圖。繫之以僞跋。眞跋繫之以僞圖。此出市井小人之所爲巧計。日久知一落於此。一落於彼。彼此爭持。而不肯合。此大煞風景。

XII 集書畫成錄者。或僅記人名圖數。或并詳其題款。自宣和書畫譜始。繼之以畫繼。王氏書苑畫苑。書畫錄。朱性甫鐵網珊瑚。都南濠鐵網珊瑚。清河書畫舫。寶繪錄。眞蹟日錄。圖繪寶鑑。無聲詩史。古今法書。名畫題跋。珊瑚網（汪砢玉）。書畫題跋記（郁逢慶）。銷夏記（陳午亭）。銷夏錄（高江邨）。銷夏錄所錄。皆觸目琳琅。客有見余輯殘編斷簡而哂之者。余曰。子何見之淺。余豈與之角勝哉。亦一時之寄興焉耳。臺閣之人。己之勢與力已足以致。而又往來於名公鉅卿間。所見益多。如朱性甫輩亦寒士也。生當弘治正德之時。遺迹尚有留落人間。一時往還者。如沈啓南文徵仲父子。皆具一世之巨眼。而又善於物色。故窮搜大而入龍宮。寶藏所見。亦非凡品。余生搜羅既盡之時。又鮮聲應氣求之友。雖年二十以外。絕意名利。即藉以消磨歲月。迄今往來於荒江寂寞之濱。又三十餘年。所見不過如是。生非其時。處非其地。非余之知識有不及于前輩諸公也。

XIII 凡物必求盡美。必爲造物所忌。必求奇異。必歸於僞妄而止。不獨書畫然也。余大父侍御公。先嚴儒林公。生於康熙初年。與韓慕廬吳西齋湯西厓何義門諸先生。務爲經濟之學。亦未嘗不游心於書畫玩器。每得宋搨法帖一二行。卽寶藏之。不問其前後也。知古人之用筆用意。餘可類而推已。 有蕭齋之遺意焉。 古玉一角。古銅一片。 已如見太古意味。無窮摩挲。 不忍釋手。但究其從何器損下。製于何代。昔之士大夫在於稽古。不在於貨利。 今求三代玉器。顏色要白。 甘黃甘靑。志有不足。血侵必紅。四散布置。物大而全。則以新玉製就。提紅油而已矣。求三代銅器。必夏鼎商彞。要五色咸備。而且鮮明。又不剝落。則以新銅鑄成燒斑而已矣。論磁必柴汝官哥。必花器香器釉足而光澤。則赴江西。照古式新燒。以砂水扡漿擦退其光而已。論書畫必要晉唐始。而宋元止。兼取紙白絹美。則捉筆揮灑而已。此外無他法也。

XIV 收藏印非妄下也。有一定之步位。宜大宜小。宜朱文宜白文。無可容則可已矣。詩與跋非妄作也。詩有意旨。跋有發明。字之大小。或草或楷。俱有恰當。往往敷衍幾句。 則又何必。非如生員歲試。 勒令必到也。前明之犯此病者。 在在皆是。何况今日。 余不自量。輒爲人下筆。然總於別紙。日後聽其去留可也。

XV 張守中桃花山鳥名畫也。銷夏錄載之。近歸吳中一人。愛之甚。藏之深。有裝池而居吳者最狡黠。同郡一宦。每過其店。輒譽是畫。黠者因至藏畫家。說以畫本日久漿退紙縐。卷舒必爲害。須加以薄漿。直而藏之可無恙。因信其言而付之。即倩人摹成一幅。料宦者來。以眞本貼於壁之高處。宦果至曰。此物何出也。曰玩久生厭。將重裝。照原價而售矣。宦曰。原價吾所知也。斯畫吾所欲也。黠者曰。予可無利而空行乎。宦者曰。必有以酬之。歸而取價。黠者易僞者貼於壁之高處。須臾宦至。交價及酬。黠者故令人喚藏畫家之僕至。僕亦僞爲受其價。而存其酬。起畫磨好裝成。交宦。而事畢矣。眞者仍還原所。後宦覺而無可如何矣。

XVI 近有一人善作僞本。一人又出本數金。囑造各種畫。極意裝池。忽作僞者之筆墨。人人看破。其法不行。出本定做者無從銷售矣。邇代貴官收買物件。謂之辦差。又一盲於目而盲於心者。執是役。欲以售。彼復慮倩人看出。吳中有一典鋪。時當書畫。出本者至其典。挽通典中櫃夥。將僞物畢置是處。空出當票一紙。抬前其年月。出本者持票而告盲於心者曰。某家積有古物。茲不能守。君所知也。某典之善於捆絕人物。而不出。君所知也。今某家之物。悉入某典。而何時出。君長者其圖之。票在是。盲於心者曰。我其備本利而贖之。物佳再找。否則已矣。出本者曰善。悉如君命。遂贖而墮其術。

XVII 吾友好弄書畫玩器。頗有蓄。而眞僞參半。屢爲人打換。忽去忽來。瞬息而案頭俱僞矣。又有收而復賣。賣而又收。久之銀盡。存物甚多。而不能賣銀矣。

XVIII 曾見一人。飲後至骨董鋪。囊中有銀。店主覘知。見其時取盤中一僞玉圈撫摩。店主察其神情。認爲玉矣。因巧言出其囊銀而賣之。歸醒而覺。一言不出。越半年。是端陽前數日。前醉者同一山西人。至以石作玉之店。出鍾馗一幅寄售。索價二十金。店主曰。不必存矣。量值僅兩許。而何廿爲。前醉者曰。彼西人。烏知筆墨。趁此節中。店中張掛幾日而還之。亦有何礙。店主唯唯。張之于壁。前醉者又令一山西人數進其店。而觀斯畫曰。此敝省名人筆也。意欲要此。店主索五十金。其人願出十金。添至十六金。而將去。店主曰。此乃寄也。尙當問之。其人出一小銀錢重三錢者。爲定而去。明日前醉者同寄畫之山西人至其店。索寄物。店主收下屢還屢止。曰有人肯出三兩。鄙見亦可銷矣。寄者大笑曰。此祖傳世寶。前以少盤費而爲之。今有矣。前醉者再三勸之。有銀何患無畫。于是至十二金而成交。店主期以明日付銀。寄者曰。吾將登舟。廿人待吾。復持而走。店主忖尚餘四金。遂應之。於是僞玉之銀盡返而餘矣。

XIX 甲與乙相友。甲能書通文理。販書畫。外似憨哥。內頗詭譎。乙受業而看書畫。冀以取利。久之。甲曰。汝鑑進矣。令乙買一件。甲與售獲大利。乙素有本業。經營藥材。於是疏本業。而專務書畫。乙有所得。必質之于甲。甲曰買則買之。甲曰舍則舍之。甲持而令乙買。乙必從命。如陳相之見許行也。又久之。乙本業荒而貲本盡。書畫汗牛。無有顧問。載之遠遊。亦完璧而返。謀之甲。甲曰此待時待價而動者。何亟亟也。無如乙之貲本。盡在書畫。乙應還本業客人之貨價。亦盡在於書畫。客不能待。逼索急迫。欲以抵補於客。客視之如敝屣。若將浼焉。乙舍是無別抵。客訟於官。拘乙榜笞。繫之縲紲。追後以房屋稍償。客無如何而止。聞者每爲太息。近余至一處。賈者畢集。甲抵掌而侈貨殖之妙。余諷之曰。近見乙乎。其景況何如。甲曰是人窮極無賴矣。舉座譁然。甲去。余曰。此有一笑話也。一人行於道。見道上棄嚼乾之蔗渣。復拾入口而大嚼。毫無餘液。吐而罵曰。無廉恥。咀得如此之乾。今甲之貌乙。何以異是。

XX 余飄泊江湖。留心古人遺跡。山巔水湄。糢糊刊刻。即冒險亦必細覽。偶至一處。敗紙一堆。必反覆尋繹。冀有所得。而亦隨以採風。知其習俗。即此書畫一道。至風雅也。可悲可歎之事。已不勝舉。況其他乎。吳越爲各省必由之路。傾蓋而逢。日凡幾輩。城中古玩舖。以百計攜而銷售。俗呼之曰。捐木梢。更不可數。殆皆不講信實。斷絕一人。復有一人踵而繼。生計之易以居於吳越。花銷之易。亦以居於吳越。妓船鱗比。酒閣蟬聯。千般巧計而得之者一投足而蕩然矣。

XXI 書畫無款非病也。宋人無款而且無印者甚多。凡院本而應制者。皆無印無款。如馬夏諸公。或於下角偶於樹石之無礙處。以小楷書名。李龍眠能書而不喜書款。今人得真蹟。而必於角上添「龍眠李公麟」五字。罪大惡極。古人或書或畫。而至於不朽。其人必有宿根。鍾山川靈秀之氣而生。加之以博覽。積之以苦功。然後成此慧業。一人有一人之面目。即父子亦不相肖。如大令已不似右軍。至必傳一也。夫如是何必藉款。

善鑒者一覽。而知此種筆墨。必出某人。善鑒者非仙也。舍是人無弟二人能之者。定之總不失。作者一場辛苦而成。豈無傳意。然不書名者亦曰。後人當知非吾莫能爲也。然此後人。非言泛泛庸庸之人。一代之作書畫者。止一二人。鑒書畫者。亦止一二人。且鑒者亦必自能作者。唐之歐虞褚薛。宋之米氏父子。蘇氏父子。元之趙氏父子。柯敬仲輩。皆傳人而鑒傳跡。今則不知何許之人。街談巷議。彼所恃者。猶識得名耳。故款在所必需。

XXII 宋人書名不用印。用印不書名。見之黃山谷。暨先渭南公。

XXIII 書畫不遇名手裝池。雖破爛不堪。寧包好藏之匣中。不可壓以他物。不可性急而付拙工。性急而付拙工。是滅其蹟也。拙工謂之殺畫劊子。今吳中張玉瑞之治破紙本。沈迎文之治破絹本。實超前絕後之技。爲名賢之功臣。

XXIV 書畫之大小闊狹。本無定也。古人偶得名紙。卽興到筆隨。今則以二尺爲止。闊則八九寸爲。收無用舊畫。截小去款。另書著名宋元之人。至以巨幅。改作三四幅。命名必祥瑞。積至百數。往銷他處。余始甚爲此輩危之。越幾月見其或持銀以歸。或又帶別處之貨。售於家鄉。或以此銀。并捐小小功名。問之云。宋元人名只在數金以內。一軸。然計本已可得三倍矣。事不可料如此。

XXV　書畫祕密而藏。不與人看。自亦不看。如以大寶沈之深淵。最不可解。然輕與人觀。亦非也。其人全然不懂。徒勞卷舒。反以油手指點。吐沫噴濺。有損無益。

XXVI　名蹟全賴收藏得地。如聽蟲嚙鼠咬。或置卑溼而霉爛。其罪過與棄粥飯於污穢同。

XXVII　書畫必位置得宜。山水園林最稱。即竹籬茅舍。打掃潔淨。亦無不可。高堂華廈。金碧輝煌。反覺減色。如中懸名繪。旁列硃箋。俗字對聯。聯句則堂皇冠冕。出名則權勢赫弈。兼佐以燒斑銅鼎。孔雀毛扇。洋貨時鳴鐘等物。此書畫之阨境也。

XXVIII　賞鑑難得頭緒。如從未見其人之眞蹟。忽來一臨摹善本。則爲其所惑。如既見矣。烏得更指鹿爲馬。然此難望之無心無目之人。

XXIX　勿與門外人爭眞僞。徒費唇舌。多一物添一累。多一事不如少一事。自亦不講爲安。無奈覺得俗氣逼人。　丙申荷月朔聽松山人納涼無事而作是說。

書畫作僞日奇論

　　書畫作僞。自昔有之。往往以眞蹟置前。千臨百摹。以冀感人。卒至前生後熟。始合終離。易爲人勘破。遇一名物。題詠甚多。以一人一手出之。雖千變萬化。而一人之面目仍在。昔人惜物力。審分量。作僞不盡佳墨名紙選毫。以後代之絹楮。作前朝之書畫。破綻已先呈露。不辨而明矣。今則不用舊本臨摹。不假十分著名之人。而稍淡冷落。一以杜撰出之。反有自然之致。且無從以眞蹟刊本較對。題詠不一。雜以眞草隸篆。使不觸目。或糾合數人爲之。故示其異。藏經紙宣德紙。乃希有之物。不顧折福損壽。大書特書紙之破碎處。聽其缺裂。字以隨之不全。

　　前輩收藏家印記。及名公名號圖章。尙有流落人間者。乞假而印於隙處。金題玉躞。裝池珍重。心思之用極。而人情之薄至矣。更有異者。熟人而有本者。亦以杜撰出之。高江村銷夏錄。詳其絹楮之尺寸。圖記多寡。以絕市駔之巧計。今則悉照其尺寸而備絹楮。悉照其圖記而篆姓名。仍不對眞本。而任意揮灑。銷夏錄之原物。作僞者不得而見。收買者亦未之見。且五花八門爲之。惟冀觀於錄。而核其尺寸絲毫不爽耳。至假爲項墨林高江村之子孫。別其吳越之聲口。持僞物以售。并挖通收藏家。以物寄於其處。導人往觀。以作希眞。嗟乎。古人於立德立功立言之外。即從事於六法八法。以爲不朽之業。 今則作此欺詐。以爲嫖賭之資。 天堂事業。竟成地獄變相。如鬼如蜮。每誆到手。成百成廿。卒至飢寒。終歸烏有。何也。作僞則本心離。無本焉能立。來易去易。偕穿窬之輩。同歸於盡而止。

Other titles by R. H. van Gulik, available from Orchid Press:
Crime and Punishment in Ancient China: *T'ang-Yin-Pi-Shih*
Hayagriva: Horse Cult in Asia
Mi Fu on Ink-stones
The Lore of the Chinese Lute: An Essay in the Ideology of the Ch'in

R. H. van Gulik biography available from Orchid Press:
Dutch Mandarin: The Life and Work of R. H. van Gulik

www.ingramcontent.com/pod-product-compliance
Lightning Source LLC
Chambersburg PA
CBHW031444210526
45464CB00005B/2324